UNMASKING THE PAST

A Story of Resilience and Healing
Using the Power of Positive Thinking

SHARON WESTIN

First published by Ultimate World Publishing 2021

Copyright © 2021 Sharon Westin

ISBN
Paperback: 978-1-922597-49-6
Ebook: 978-1-922597-50-2

Sharon Westin has asserted her rights under the Copyright, Designs and Patents Act 1988 to be identified as the author of this work. The information in this book is based on the author's experiences and opinions. The publisher specifically disclaims responsibility for any adverse consequences which may result from the use of the information contained herein. Permission to use information has been sought by the author. Any breaches will be rectified in further editions of the book.

All rights reserved. No part of this publication may be reproduced, stored in or introduced into a retrieval system or transmitted in any form, or by any means (electronic, mechanical, photocopying, recording or otherwise) without the prior written permission of the author. Any person who does any unauthorised act in relation to this publication may be liable to criminal prosecution and civil claims for damages. Enquiries should be made through the publisher.

Cover design: Sharon Westin Graphic Design
Layout and typesetting: Sharon Westin Graphic Design
Editor: Rebecca Low

Disclaimer

This book contains the memories and opinions of the author. As such, some dates and places may be incorrect. The author's memories and feelings do not intend to offend, and the author does not presume to tell the story of others who feature predominantly in this book. Their feelings, emotions, thoughts and memories are their own, and they deserve the respect the author gives them by only writing about them in a way that is necessary for telling her story. This is her perspective only, and the author acknowledges that readers may have different recollections or perspectives on the persons and events recounted in this text.

The strategies used by the author do not intend to replace professional advice on mental health or other medical issues. However, if this story triggers painful memories of your own, please seek help from a professional. There is a list of services available at the end of chapters 7 and 11.

*Some names have been changed for privacy in the Gone, Daddy, Gone chapter.

To my boys, Connor and Mitchell, you have given me strength when I needed it most. I am so proud of how you have overcome obstacles of your own to become the lovely young men before me.

To Leonie, you too have a story, yet you are among the most positive people I know. You are my rock, and I honestly couldn't have survived the last five years without your endless support.

To the people trying to heal from what they won't discuss, I'm sending you hugs.
May you find your voice.

Contents

Foreword	7
Preface	9
Introduction	13
Gone, Daddy, Gone	21
Mummy Dearest	37
Home Sweet Home(less)	51
The New Kid in School	57
Sex(uality)	71
He Ain't Heavy	79
Party Like it's 1999	89
Our Rocketman	95
Sister-Not-Sister	111
An Apple A Day	115
From Negative to Positive: How I Healed Myself	125
About the Author	155
Heartfelt thanks	161

Foreword

Sharon came to me for the first time in November 2019. I remember opening the door and just feeling a broken woman. Lost and confused, her inner child was screaming out and so scared. She was stuck, unhappy and full of fear.

After one healing, her inner strength was present. Sharon started stepping out of her comfort zone and speaking up for change. She then went to a women's retreat in Fiji, which changed her forever. The clear vision and inspiration she returned with were magical.

She had an idea, and within months, was organising her own retreats, as well as running her graphic design business and art classes. Wow! She was on a mission and no one was going to stop her.

Then something quite daunting happened and she messaged me for a healing. Again, I opened the door and saw that broken, scared little girl. She had received some news through DNA testing. Her whole world, in a sense, came crashing down. After the healing, her strength was once again present.

I've seen Sharon in a broken state on several occasions, but her ability to acknowledge and feel the pain, then dust herself off and get on with what she wants to achieve is truly inspiring. Her positive attitude and easy-going personality make her an absolute delight to be around.

I'm completely gob smacked by what she has accomplished and how she has grown since our first meeting. Running retreats, writing this book, running her own businesses, and all of it done with love and laughter.

Thank you, Sharon. I look forward to working with you on future endeavours and watching your path unfold as you flow through this journey we call life.

Penny Theofanidou
Spiritual Life Coach & Healer at InsideOut Spiritual Healing

Preface

This is my story and my memories, although sometimes foggy. This book had been on my mind for some time. Recent events made the writing of it inevitable. I am an everyday, middle-aged woman, yet when I compare my past to those around me, my story is quite different. Mental health issues, tragedy, estrangement from family, profound grief, and what some may see as just plain bad luck have followed me all my life.

The last 18 months have seen me grow spiritually, and I choose not to see my past as a negative but as the universe's plan for me to be where I am today. Today, I am separated from my husband, amicably co-parenting, running three businesses, and looking for love. Today, I am strong, I am resilient, and I am calm. Today, I am a relaxed woman working towards the future I am meant to live.

I have chosen not to write about my marriage out of respect for Andrew, but I will say that he is a great dad, and I love him as my children's father. He is an active dad who participates in all aspects of the kids' lives. We share 50/50 custody, and I am very proud of him, myself, and especially our boys in how we have handled our separation.

I have also chosen not to speak specifically about my children. They are quickly growing into young men and their story is not mine to tell.

My family tree is complicated. To help you understand, I have drawn a tree and listed the prominent people below and how they all fit in.

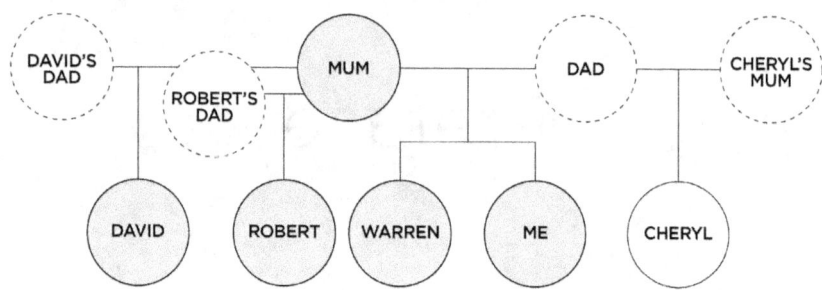

My mother – I have chosen not to use her name in this book.

My father – Ronnie.

My brothers – David (Dave), Robert (Robbie), and Warren (Wazza).

David has a different father from me and has four other half-siblings (coincidentally, one is also named Sharon). His partner was Leonie.

Robbie has a different father from me and has three other half-siblings, one only six months younger than himself. His ex-partner is Joanne.

Warren and I share a father.*

Cheryl is Ronnie's first child and was born before Warren and me.

Andrew is my ex-husband.

Connor and Mitchell are my beautiful boys.

* The introduction will clarify this.

1977 – Warren, Robbie, me and Dave.

1979 – Robbie and Dave (back). Warren and me (front).

Around 1980 – Me, Robbie, Dave, Mum and Warren in front of 'our' tree in Dandenong, Victoria. The photographer got Warren to smile by getting him to press the music button on his watch.

2003 – Robbie and Dave (back), Mum and me (front) at our tree on Mother's Day.

2009 – Me with my boys, Mitchell and Connor, at our tree on Mother's Day.

2009 – Joanne, Robbie, me, Mum, Andrew, Leonie and Dave at our tree on Mother's Day.

2005 – Me, pregnant with Connor, with Andrew at our home in Oakleigh East.

Buddy, our adorable Maltese Shih Tzu.

2016 – Andrew, Connor, Mitchell and me in Vernazza, Cinque Terre, Italy, after a two-hour hike along the cliff face.

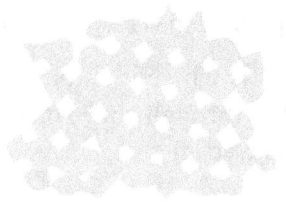

Introduction

The DNA results were complete. I was so keen to find out my heritage breakdown to see if it was similar to my newfound half-sister's. I never knew I had Swedish heritage until I met Cheryl, and for some reason, I wanted to do this test to cement my connection with her. We had already formed a strong bond, and this test would reaffirm our sisterhood.

I excitedly clicked on the link in the email.

Hold on…is this the correct result? Have they sent me someone else's DNA results? There must be a mistake. I am confused. Am I reading this correctly? There was no Sweden in the little pie chart showing my heritage. Only Ireland (33%), England (33%), Scotland (31%), and Wales (3%). Where was the automatic link to Cheryl and my dad's brother?

I took a screenshot and sent it to Cheryl along with the comment, "WTF?"

As I waited for Cheryl's response, I investigated further. For those unfamiliar with DNA results provided by ancestry.com.au, the dashboard splits into three sections:

- DNA Story – where you can see your Ethnicity Estimate
- DNA Matches – this is where it automatically shows the people who you are linked to through your DNA, as they have also done the test through this website
- ThruLines™ – this shows you how you may be related to your DNA matches through common ancestors.

In my DNA matches, I had 310 fourth cousins or closer. I was fascinated, yet still confused. The first person on the list under the heading 'Close Family' was a first-second cousin. I recognised the name. It was one of my cousin's children on my mum's side of the family. OK, this was my DNA... I didn't know the other two under this heading. The second person, a second-third cousin, had a linked family tree, but I didn't recognise any names shown. The third, also a second-third cousin, had a linked tree, but it was private. The following heading showed 'Extended Family'. As I scanned the list, I started to see some family names from my mum's side.

Cheryl should have come up in my DNA matches near the top of my 'Close Family.' She didn't, and neither did my uncle. What did this mean? I had waited over 30 years to find Cheryl, and now, through the wonder of DNA, I found out we were not half-sisters after all because I am not related to the man I grew up knowing to be my dad.

This revelation left me light-headed. I still couldn't believe what I was reading and needed to do more investigation. In haste, I started randomly looking through the 'Extended Family' list and clicked on anyone who had a linked tree. It became clear that many relatives on my mum's side of the family had done the DNA test. As I clicked on these trees, I could start building my digital family tree. I spent many hours putting pieces of my family puzzle together. I realised I hadn't checked the first person in the 'Extended Family' section in my haze of confusion. I clicked on their linked tree.

"What. The. Fuck?" I said aloud, although no one was there to hear me. There was a name I recognised. It was the uncommon surname of my eldest brother Dave's father. Let me note, the name wasn't in Dave's father's generation, but from someone born in 1922. It then repeated back through three more generations in this family tree. The exact first name and surname. Did this mean Dave was my full brother and not my half-brother? So then, Warren was not my full brother, but my half-brother? I honestly never questioned whether my dad was my dad. I thought we looked similar...

At that moment, in getting my DNA results, I:

- lost a dad
- potentially gained a dad (therefore another four half-siblings, including the other Sharon!)
- lost a full-blood brother
- potentially gained a full-blood brother
- lost a half-sister who only found me a few months ago.

Again...WTF!?!

I quickly shot off a message to two of my mum's sisters to see if they had any knowledge of this. They didn't. One aunt offered to call my mum. You see, by my choice, I hadn't seen or talked to my mum for 12 years. My aunt promptly called my mum, asking her about this newly uncovered skeleton, and then called me back. My aunt told me that my mum said that Ronnie was my dad and the DNA test was a joke. She then yelled and swore at my aunt and told her never to contact her again. After my aunt relayed the conversation she had with my mum, I apologised to her for dealing with that on my behalf. It's not the first time I have apologised to someone for my mum's behaviour.

Messenger pinged on my phone. It was Cheryl. "Not Swedish??? Not related to me??? WTF!!! Bizarre!!! It linked me straight away. I'll call you tonight..."

Needing a break, I called my sister-in-law Leonie to tell her what I discovered. We talked for almost an hour, figuring out why my mum would lie to me about this. How could my mum deceive not only me but my 'dad,' my brothers, and our extended family? Like me, Leonie was shocked but not surprised. My mum had lied to my two eldest brothers about who their dads were, so why wouldn't she lie about mine?

Leonie did tell me something I never knew, though, which made the mystery surrounding my father even more compelling. After Dave reunited with his father, his father said to him that our mum once told him he fathered two of her children, both boys, and that one had died in a motorbike accident. Dave immediately shot him down, saying that it can't be true as Robbie now knew his dad, and Warren and I were definitely Ronnie's children, and none of us had died in a motorbike accident. Well, Dave, he may have been telling the truth, or at least what he thought to be the truth. Leonie gave me Dave's father's phone number. I didn't have any other option but to call him. It was already late, so I decided to wait until the next day to call. My head was spinning.

I have spoken to this man once before. It was in 2016, and I called to tell him that Dave had died. I tried the number a couple of times, and on the third try, he answered. It was 5 pm on a Friday, and he was at the golf club with friends. I got straight to the point. I introduced myself as Dave's sister and said I understood that he had fathered two of my mum's kids. He repeated what Leonie told me, and I told him that was untrue and that I thought I was the other child. He was surprised but seemed to take the call quite well and continued in his calm manner. It almost felt like he expected the phone call.

We chatted for around 10 minutes, going through my DNA results, his name coming up in my DNA matches, and the timeline when he knew my mum. He seemed to think it didn't quite line up. At this point, a thought popped into my head. I asked if he had a brother. He did, but he passed away at the age of 28. In my mind, this didn't discount him. I asked if he would consider doing a DNA test, and he said he would have to talk it over with his wife and get back to me. He ended the conversation by saying that he would like to meet me if I were his daughter. After the call, I felt good. I felt optimistic that this could be the answer I was now searching for.

I gave him a week and sent a text message to follow up. Unfortunately, I didn't have it in me to call. The days after I got my results, I was an emotional mess. For three days, I cried, researched DNA, re-checked my results over and over again, and spoke to a few close friends. Thank god for those friends! I knew these results didn't change who I was, my friends reassured me of that, but it was an unknown in my life that I needed to resolve. I hoped Dave's dad would give me that answer. Days later, he finally responded and said he wouldn't do the test. Dead end...

Two days later, on a whim and as I waited to meet a friend at a café, I rang my mum. I thought this call could end in a few ways. She would a) hang up immediately b) scream at me and then hang up c) soften once she heard my voice and tell me the truth, or d) talk to me and continue with the lies of the past. D. She chose to believe her lies, continually told me what a silly woman I was for even doing the DNA test, that I was such a terrible person for spreading these rumours, and then went on to say how much I have hurt her for depriving her of her grandchildren for 12 years. She threw blame at me for her broken heart, for my brother Robbie's mental state, and for not telling her Dave was sick.

She honestly couldn't understand why I would think she had lied to me about my dad. Could it be that she had told Dave that his dad had died (untrue) or that she never told Robbie who his dad was (he met him in 2003, or thereabouts, after a chance encounter between his half-brother and one of our aunts)? Or could it be that I have been lied to so many times by her throughout my life that it seemed plausible to me? I remained calm throughout this conversation and called her out for many things that had upset me over the years. After she complained about being all alone, she went on to say that all she wanted was for everyone to leave her alone. I ended the call by saying it would be the last time she heard from me. I cried and shook, and went into the café and ordered a Bloody Mary. It was 10 am on a Sunday.

A few days later, I asked Leonie if one of her kids could do a DNA test to see if I were a half-aunt or a full-aunt. This way, I could gain more clarity about whether Dave's dad was my dad. Dave and Leonie's eldest child Katelyn kindly offered to do the test. We waited a couple of months for the results to come in. I was excited when I got the message that the results were in, but again, I was disappointed. Half-aunty...

Being a half-aunty to Dave and Leonie's kids is merely a biological fact. As with my brothers, my nieces and nephews are my blood and I love them. The test result hasn't changed the way I feel about them.

REFLECTIONS

Throughout this roller coaster, every person I spoke with said, "Your life could be a Netflix series," or "You should write a book." So, here I am, writing my first book. This moment is just one in my life that will forever change me. I have had many. More than most people I know. It's been tough, but it has made me the person I am today. I wanted to share these stories to show you that when life gets all 'lifey,' there are ways to help yourself. There are ways to overcome your struggles, down moments, and darkness, and I want to share what I have done to heal myself. It's taken time and consistency, and I will always be on a path of healing. Still, I am happier than I have been in a long time, thanks to permitting myself to let go of the victim mindset and finally begin to heal with the help of positive thoughts. I am now comfortable sitting with my emotions, letting them pass through me and moving on.

What is a victim mindset?

The victim mindset is a personality trait that makes you feel like the victim of circumstance or others' actions. The feeling of 'woe is me,' 'bad luck follows me,' 'I never win'…you get the picture. This mindset was ingrained in me through years of negative talk and action surrounding me. It was my norm. If something went wrong, it was expected rather than a misfortune. I would often go over the worst-case scenario, so I was prepared for what I anticipated was to come. That's not the way I wanted to live. It's not the way anyone should live.

How did I let go of the victim mindset?

I now realise that I was carrying on the negativity cycle that I had grown up with. What I was putting out into the universe was coming back tenfold. I wasn't taking responsibility for my life and happiness. I allowed the adverse events and situations to continually control my thoughts and often analysed every situation, rather than constructively work through the emotions it brought up in me and work through them.

After my eldest brother Dave's death, I began to feel a shift within me. I decided to focus more on myself and how I reacted and found calm within. I now understand that my parent's pain and dysfunction are not mine to carry, and the events in my life happened around me, not to me. I have finally released myself from the feelings of not being good enough, of not belonging, the constant need to be loved (although still a work in progress), and realised that my behaviour needed to change. The cycle stops here. I am real, I am raw, I am authentic, and I am so damn proud of myself now!

The last chapter of this book will detail the strategies I have used to rediscover who I am and yet to become, and I hope you find the tools helpful in your own life. There are also questions for you to answer to get you started on your journey.

Here's to new beginnings, no matter what stage of your life you are in.

> We all have a story. The difference is: do you use the story to empower yourself? Or do you use your story to keep yourself a victim? The question itself empowers you to change your life.
>
> – Sunny Dawn Johnston

Ethnicity Estimate

● Ireland	33% >
● England & Northwestern Europe	33% >
● The Midlands, England	>
● The Potteries	
● Scotland	31% >
● Wales	3% >

Close Family

Katelyn	Half niece 898 cM | 13% shared DNA Mother's side	⚡ Public linked tree 25 People 🍃 Common ancestor

Screen shots from my DNA profile on ancestry.com.au.

Chapter 1

Gone, Daddy, Gone

Growing up in a single-parent family, I had various father figures in my life over the years. Of some, I have only faded memories. However, I always felt different around my friends' families, whose parents were all still married. I loved seeing the dynamics within their homes and longed for that in my own home, with my own father.

Ronnie

My dad left when I was two. I don't know why he left or the reasons behind my parents' separation and subsequent divorce.

One of the first memories I have of my dad is when I lived in Dingley. I was seven years old. He brought his German Shepherd named Lady to come and pick us up one day. She was big, and I was scared of her. Nonetheless, I was happy to be spending time with the dad I didn't know. I am not sure why I hadn't seen him for so long, but here we were, spending school holidays with him. Warren and I would drive with him to Ararat and stay with his mum, brother, aunt, cousin, and her family. I don't know how we all fit in the tiny house!

It was an old, red-brick building. I remember walking around the front of the house and running my finger along the brick, which was powdery and falling off at my touch. My grandmother was old and short, with a shock of white hair. I remember her being kind but not overly affectionate. Their toilet was an outhouse that mortified me. Going outside in the dark to pee was not my favourite thing, and I would rush out and do my business as fast as possible before running back inside. I was constantly scared that I would get bitten by a spider or kidnapped in the dark.

We would go to the pub during these holidays where we ate pork crackle from a packet and learned to play pool while my dad drank at the bar. We would play in the backyard, often counting the freight trains' carriages that went past the back of the property or sit in Dad's car playing on the CB radio. Other times we would go shooting and yabbying. Upon returning from yabbying, we would eat the fresh catch dipped in vinegar and pepper. The rabbits caught were stewed, and I recall the kitchen's horrible smell. I haven't eaten rabbit since and doubt I ever will again. On one of the shooting trips, Dad gave me the gun to shoot my first rabbit. The rabbit was already wounded, so it was easy for me to hit. It was an awful feeling, and I vowed never to intentionally hurt an animal again.

While out in the paddocks during some of these trips, Dad would let Warren drive an old car with me as a passenger. I was not allowed to be at the wheel, but on one occasion, Warren let me. Dad didn't know, of course. So I started driving with Warren as my instructor, and I went up the side of a dam. Unfortunately, the dam's edge was quite steep, and I ended up driving the vehicle around it at a 45-degree angle. If Warren hadn't grabbed the steering wheel, the car would have rolled. It scared us enough never to do it again. I was nine years old.

Warren and I spent a lot of time sitting in Dad's car while he fixed it. I remember it was a white car. I've never been good at remembering makes and models, and it doesn't matter, but I know Warren would remember every detail, loving cars the way he did. A blue 'wife-beater' singlet and shorts were Dad's everyday attire, and he was rarely without a VB stubby and cigarette in hand, no matter what we were doing. Warren and I would listen to the CB radio or Bruce Springsteen's *Born in the USA* album on cassette. I would repeatedly read the lyrics and still sing along word for word when I hear them on the radio.

Very late one evening, we drove to the local asylum to steal vegetables from their garden. Not quite the holiday activity I expected. Just like on this night, I have so many memories of Dad holding the wire of a barbed-wire fence for me to climb through. I can still feel the sting on my skin when I didn't quite make it through without touching it.

Other visits with Dad included a trip to the Grampians. Unfortunately, I didn't have appropriate footwear for hiking, and as Dad, Warren, and I crossed a river by jumping from rock to rock, I slipped and fell, landing hip-first onto one of them. I had some coins in the pocket of my light pink shorts and remembered the mark left. You could almost make out what denomination they were.

My only other memory of spending time with Dad during this time was at his home in Dandenong. It was a run-down house, which I now consider a council house. There was a party with lots of adults and kids. Warren and I didn't know anyone, but we ran around all night playing tiggy with the other kids. Unfortunately, I rolled my ankle on an extension cord, and when an adult fetched my dad, he was so drunk he started rubbing the wrong ankle.

I was nine years old when I stopped seeing my dad. I don't remember any event that caused these visits to stop, and I don't recall Mum telling us why we couldn't see him anymore. So, life went back to just Mum and us kids. I received birthday cards with money in them for a few years, but eventually, they stopped.

I didn't see Dad again until March 1997, when I was 20. My family drove to Ararat for my grandmother's funeral. I was nervous and anxious. When we arrived, people were milling about out the front of the old red-brick house. I didn't recognise anyone, and it wasn't until I got out of the car that I saw him. My body started to shake, and I began crying. I couldn't control it. After so many years, the physical effect of seeing him was challenging for me to understand. He came straight over and said, "Hello. You've grown up beautiful." I said thank you and walked away. I didn't know what to do or say. Even if I had the words, it wasn't the right time to talk.

At 20 years of age, I felt so mature and street smart, yet at that moment, I was a sad little girl who missed her dad. I have yearned for the love and affection of a father my entire life. Someone to look up to, someone to hold me, someone to rely on, someone to love me, someone to be proud of the woman I had become. In my mind, from all my mum had told me, my dad was a worthless man who didn't deserve my love. With this in mind, when he called me out of the blue on my 21st birthday later that year, I said, "Thank you for calling, but I would prefer if you didn't call me again." That was the last time I spoke to my dad. My mum didn't allow him to come to Warren's funeral four weeks earlier.

Dad died of lung cancer in 2012. I was working when Dave rang and told me the news. I burst into tears. Again, I was shocked at the way this affected me. I cried on and off for the rest of the day. I think it was a deep sadness, knowing I would never have the opportunity to repair our relationship, nor have the chance to ask him why. Why did he leave me all those years ago? Why didn't he fight to see me? Why did he go on and be a stepdad to other children but not have time for me? I will never find out the answer to those questions, so I had to find a way to move on.

REFLECTIONS

Like any grief, time helps but doesn't heal. The healing happened when I finally understood that I wasn't the reason Dad left. His leaving didn't necessarily mean he didn't love me, and I eventually became okay with that. Now, the revelation that he wasn't my biological father has brought up other emotions. I feel sad that he never knew, and feel sad that he was lied to, as were all of my family and his. As with all lies, the ripple effect of my DNA test results will continue until I find out the truth, which realistically may never happen. Am I okay with that? I'm not sure, to be honest, but I know it's just another speed bump in my life that I will manage to get across.

If she could put the hollow ache that haunts her into words, she would tell him, "I miss the father you never were."

– John Mark Green

Dad and me at our home in Endeavour Hills before he left.

Me with Dad's dog Lady, out the front of our home in Dingley around 1985.

Around 1985 – Me, Dad, and Warren at the Grampians, Victoria.

Robbie, Dad, Dave (back), me and Warren (front) in the front yard of Grandma's.

Me out the front of Grandma's house in Ararat.

Dad, me, Uncle Kevin, and Warren on one of our yabbying trips.

Me, visibly upset at Grandma's funeral, after seeing my dad for the first time in 11 years. This is one of the last photos I know of with Warren (in the background) before his death.

Christian*

I thought Christian was so exotic, but looking back with adult eyes, I think he was just a European stoner. The acrid smell of marijuana is one of the first things I remember when I think of him. I had my first kiss at Christian's house. I was six. We used tongue, and I remember stealing kisses when no one watched. I think the boy was Christian's nephew; I really can't remember. I didn't see him again. Thinking back, I don't know why we kissed in such a grown-up manner. Wasn't that supposed to happen in your teens? Maybe it was because I was privy to sexuality from an early age. I was at Christian's house one day with my mum. One of Christian's friends was also there. Mum told me to stay in the kitchen, but I snuck out when I heard strange noises. There was a bedroom on a mezzanine, and all three adults were there. I couldn't see, but I can only now understand what I heard was a sexual encounter. I may be wrong, but I have always been quite astute. My instincts have always been strong and usually correct.

Tim*

Tim stayed around long enough for me to call him Dad. Mum told me in later years that he told me off for calling him Dad. My mind's eye can see Tim and Mum in their art gallery and shop – paintings everywhere, the smell of turps and oil paints filling the air. I felt that my mum was happy here in her element.

Once, when Tim was babysitting me, he had to run some errands. I don't know what suburb we drove to, but it was an industrial area. I remember many brick buildings with roller doors like you'd see at a mechanic's. Tim told me to wait in the car; he wouldn't take long. He left me for two hours. I was around four or five years old. I got out of the car because I needed to go to the toilet and burst into tears because I didn't know where he was. I was petrified. He must have heard me because he came out and was angry at me for getting out of the car. That is my first memory of feeling absolute fear. I thought he'd left me and there was nobody around to help me.

Another gold star moment from Tim was at the local swimming pool. This time I was around five or six. There was a massive, enclosed water slide that my brothers went on many times over. I was desperate to try it but was too scared. It was so big looking up at it. If I were to look at it now, I would laugh at how small it is! Finally, Tim persuaded me to try the slide, promising that he would be in the pool to catch me when I whooshed out. He was there, but instead of catching me, he laughed as he let me fall deep into the water. I can still hear the sound of the rush of water on the slide as I sped out that day. I love being in or near the water, but I am scared if I am in even slightly rough water. I am sure that's the root of the fear.

Mum and Tim's relationship didn't last. I was too young to know what went on here, but I recall how scared I was when Tim drove off in his blue van, Mum chasing him, pulling on the windscreen wipers and cutting her hand.

John*

I am not sure how they met, but my mum started a relationship with John, an aircraft engineer, before moving from Endeavour Hills to Dingley. He helped us move, and we were closer to his home and his work at Moorabbin Airport by moving there. This house move meant a change of school for us all. Dave went on to Keysborough Tech, Robbie to Coomoora High School, and Warren and I to Kingswood Primary School.

John seemed classy to me. He was well-spoken, drove a Rover, and always dressed well. We spent a lot of time at the airport on weekends – the hangar smelt like a mechanic's workshop with the addition of avgas. I loved being there, watching the planes take off and land, as well as the freedom of wandering around the hangar and riding our bikes around the airport. We also had the luxury of going with John when he would take the aircraft out for a test flight. We didn't go for Sunday drives; we went for Sunday flights. I felt so free up there but didn't like the popping of my ears! When we drove past the airport, you could see the logo Mum created emblazoned on the hangar door. I was proud of her when I saw that.

When John came over, our house was always clean, well, cleanish. It's one of the only times in my childhood that I remember our house being consistently clean. Mum would make John toast and a cuppa every morning, and I would eat the leftover toast for breakfast. Jam and vegemite on cold triangles of toast.

John had a mistress, and Mum knew about it. So one day, she drove there with Warren and me in the car and parked behind his immaculate 1970s brown Rover. I can still see her at the lady's front door, yelling. I don't know what was said, but as we left in our beat-up, old, blue Mazda, she reversed, and rather than pull out into the street, she drove straight up the back of the Rover. She then moved back again, pulled out, and crashed up its side. We were scared. The sound of metal against metal was so loud. She drove to the front of the car and then proceeded to reverse into it before taking off. Our car clunked the whole way home. We passed one of Dave's friend's houses as we neared our court, where he was out the front with a group of mates. When they saw us, they ran after us, to our home, to see what on earth had happened. Our car was beaten up before, but now, it barely held together. Somehow, their relationship mended. The car didn't.

In 1988, four years after we moved to Dingley, John was offered, and accepted, a job for the Royal Flying Doctor Service as their aircraft engineer in the remote town of Derby in far, north Western Australia. He asked Mum to marry him and move there as well. Dave found a roommate and moved out. Robbie was doing his HSC and went to live with a couple so he could finish it. Warren and I had to go with Mum. Warren was in year eight, and I was in grade six.

My best friend Bee organised a surprise going-away party at her house before we left. I can picture opening the doors to her rumpus room with my other friends waiting inside. Bee gave me a silver bracelet with a small heart. It had a letter B engraved on one side of the heart, and the other side had an S. I cherished that bracelet.

In early May, Mum, Warren, our dog Oggie and myself left on what would be the most extraordinary adventure. It took us 11 days to travel by road from Melbourne to Derby, driving approximately nine hours every day. We stopped at Coober Pedy and experienced an underground church and then the underground home of Crocodile Harry. He was a creepy man who let people sign their names in paint on his walls. He only offered showers to the women. Dirty old man!!

We travelled straight up the middle of Australia, stopping at Uluru, then know as Ayers Rock. Keep in mind that this trip was well before we knew it to be such a sacred site. Warren and I were allowed to climb it and went up alone as Mum had done it on a previous trip. We shared a can of coke on the way up; no water for us in the outback heat! The sheer vastness of our country became apparent to me that day. Besides Kata Tjuta (the Olgas), there was flat red earth as far as the eye could see in every direction. After descending the rock, we walked around the base and read the plaques memorialising the people who had fallen and died. I'm glad I read that after climbing and not before.

From here, we started to make our way to Alice Springs, only to break down 100kms south of town. It was the middle of the day, and we were on a straight road that disappeared in the hot haze on the horizon. Oggie dog lay under the car to keep cool, and Warren and I tried to stay in what shade we could find beside the vehicle. We saw a car approaching and were so relieved. Our relief quickly faded as they drove straight past us, no concern for us whatsoever. Another car came along about an hour later. It was an American couple on holiday. I couldn't believe they had a mobile phone. Remember the big brick phones from the 1980s? For those too young to remember, we called them brick phones for a reason. They were massive!

The kind tourists let us call for help. Another hour later, the Outback Vehicle Recovery truck arrived and took us and our broken-down car to Alice Springs. Next to the mechanics was a camel farm. As we waited for the mechanic to let us know what the problem was and how long it would take to fix it, Warren and I went for a ride on one of the camels. I was so scared. Warren sat on the back, and I was on the front, so when the camel got up or lay down, it felt like I was going to go headfirst into the dirt. Thankfully, I didn't.

We spent three days in Alice Springs waiting for the mechanic to repair the car. I only remember a couple of things from this town: the most delicious garlic prawns I had ever tasted and coming back to our hotel room to find an enormous lizard on our door. We had to get help so we could get back into our room.

On we drove. Warren drove a lot during this trip, at only 14 years old. He took such pride in helping Mum in this way and loved every second of it. Thankfully, he wasn't driving when our car passed a road train that flicked a rock up and put a significant crack in our windscreen. I was so grateful to have been sitting in the back seat when it happened because it made us all jump – Warren most of all because it was right in his eyesight. The crack didn't stop us like the breakdown, and we continued to Daly Waters. I remember this place since it was only a pub in the middle of nowhere. We stopped at most pubs along the way for a lemon squash, but we stayed at this one overnight. Foreigners covered the walls with their banknotes, and staff added postcards from overseas tourists that had visited. Out the front stood the pub's gatekeeper, a friendly caramel-coloured cow named Daisy.

The publican told us about a safe swimming hole we could visit. We always had to be sure we only went to swimming holes recommended by locals due to the risk of being attacked by a crocodile. Warren and I sat on the front bumper as we drove down a bumpy, dirt track. Our dog was sitting in the front seat before she jumped out of the moving car's window, landing on her head and bolting from the shock. Once we found her and brushed off the red dirt, Warren and I sat back in the car. All we could think is she wanted to be with us. We arrived at the watering hole and were quite shocked at its size. It was more like a lake. Muddy, but refreshing.

After a night in less than desirable beds, we continued north, stopping at the Mataranka pub. Mum had swum in the beautiful water here, and that was our plan too. Fortunately, we stopped at the pub first as the publican told us crocs now infested it. We had a quick look anyway – it was like a desert oasis, lush and beautiful – before continuing to our next stop, Katherine. Visiting Katherine Gorge was a highlight of the trip. I had never seen anything like it. Every Australian should experience the beauty of this part of our country. The vibrant red dirt gets under your skin, and the brilliant blue of the sky makes a picture-perfect landscape. Along the walk, there were small ponds. One was quite a way down, and Oggie slipped, but we managed to catch her. There were crocs in this one, and if she fell, we would have lost her.

Looking at Australia's map, we had driven from near Adelaide, right up the centre, and took a left turn at Katherine. We were on the home stretch. John met us at Kununurra, where he took over the driving. Heading southwest, we passed through Fitzroy Crossing and arrived at our new home in Derby at midnight. It was still 25 degrees. I was so tired when we arrived, I missed my mouth when taking a sip of my drink and spilled Ribena down my pale purple top.

Our new home was the only house directly across the road from the airport. It doesn't exist anymore, I discovered after looking on Google Earth. It was a small, white, weatherboard, three-bedroom house on stilts and had a cyclone shelter out the back that we were fortunate enough not to have to use. The bathroom and toilet were attached to the house, but you had to go through the back door to get to them. Often, before going to the bathroom – and almost every time before having a shower – we had to get rid of the frogs or geckos that occupied them.

We encountered all sorts of creatures at this house. I was sent to get the washing off the line after dinner one night and ran back inside after finding an owl on the clothesline, staring at me. Another frightening encounter happened when Mum and John were out for dinner one evening. Warren and I let Oggie out for a toilet break when she started barking. We ran out to see a large, wild, black cat. She chased it through a hole in the fence out into the vast mudflats behind our house. We were screaming her name and couldn't see which direction she ran. Finally, after a heart-pounding ten minutes or so, she came back unharmed.

Those same mudflats were somewhat of a playground for Warren and me. The cracked earth went on as far as your eye could see, out into the rippling haze on the horizon. On the other side of a fence, to the right, was a bushy area that we would often see a group of wild brumbies gallop past. When I think of them, I almost see them in slow motion, like in a movie. Bored one day, Warren and I took some books and toys out to the mudflats. Being a teenage boy, Warren thought it would be fun to pick some mud up and throw it at the circling kites (a bird of prey, similar to an eagle) above us. He hit one kite, not on purpose, and the kite began swooping at us. In the air, they look big, but as this bird swooped, its massive size became apparent. You have never seen two kids run faster. We left everything out there, thongs and all, and bolted barefoot back to the safety of our house.

The airport was nine kilometres out of town. Warren and I had another adventure, riding into town one day. We stopped and played at the Boab Prison Tree on the way. This hollow tree has a circumference of over 14 metres, with a tall, narrow opening, and is said to have housed indigenous Australian prisoners in the 1890s. However, there is no evidence of this. We then ventured into town and down a road to the Derby cemetery. Not much to see here, but we had never been. Our round trip that day was around 21kms.

Not long before Mum, Warren, and I left Derby, and possibly, for this reason, I was in my room and heard a disturbance. I came out to the kitchen to find John standing over Mum, holding her by the wrists, with her bent backwards over the kitchen table. She was crying, and he was angry. I don't know what they had argued about, but we packed up and left soon after. All I could think about was the school camp to visit the dolphins at Monkey Mia and the book club order I was going to miss. Such is the mind of an 11-year-old. Somewhere around this time – I'm fuzzy on the timeline here – Mum and I went to see a lady out of town. She was a social worker, and I think she helped us move away. Mum didn't work in Derby, so I imagine the social worker helped us financially.

We flew to Perth, where we stayed in a hotel for around two weeks. Mum made many phone calls during this time, and Warren and I had to leave the room for each one. We would sit on the stairs near our room and joked that we should name the stairs one day because we were out there so often. Then, again, not knowing what was ahead of us, we flew back to Melbourne. We never saw John again.

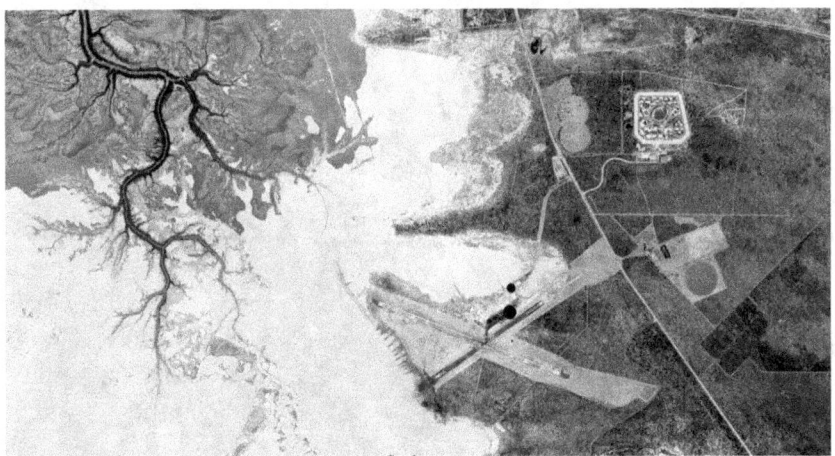

Derby Airport. The small black dot is where our house once stood. Photo source: Google Maps.

REFLECTIONS

There were more partners in my mum's life after this, but they didn't stay around long enough to feel like father figures to me. As you read in the introduction, I am not 100% sure who my dad is and may never find out. I don't necessarily need to know who he is in the hope of a relationship, because let's face it, I don't know what it's like having a father in my life. However, I feel like I need to know where I came from for my sense of self and medical history. I have two boys who may need to be aware of any hereditary issues. If I were to meet my birth father and a relationship blossomed, that would be nice, I guess, but I am not holding out for that to happen.

As a child, you are not at fault for your parents' separation. Adult issues are going on behind the scenes that you wouldn't have understood at the time and may never know because it was their relationship with each other, not their relationship with you, that caused the family breakdown.

Not all families are idealistic nuclear families with two parents and two kids. Mine was far from it. I now look at what I call my family swamp, not tree, and think, 'What an interesting story I have!' Of course, I would have loved having a dad around to love me and guide me, but my upbringing has created the person I am today.

Me and Warren out the front of Crocodile Harry's house in Coober Pedy.

Above: Me and Warren in a hollow on the side of Uluru in 1988.

Left: Me on top of Uluru in 1988, when it was still deemed acceptable to climb.

Me with Daisy out the front of the Daly Waters pub.

Warren, Oggie, and me with our broken down car, 100kms south of Alice Springs.

Warren and me riding a camel as we waited for our car to be looked at by a mechanic in Alice Springs. Warren looks so happy here. I was petrified!

Chapter 2

Mummy Dearest

I will start by saying that I love my mum, and I will always be grateful to her for doing the best she could as a single parent with what she had at the time. She showed me how to be a strong woman, and that has held me in good stead over the years through all the trials and tribulations you will read about in this book. She also encouraged my creativity from an early age. On the flip side of this, and of my choosing, I have not seen or spoken to my mum since 2008. That is until I called her recently about my DNA test result.

Mum was the sixth child and fifth daughter of Ron and Isabel. They went on to have another daughter. From what I understand, they moved around a lot. But, without going into detail because it's not my story to tell, Mum's childhood, along with her siblings, was less than desirable.

My mum gave birth to Dave in January 1969, at the age of 16. In July 1970, to a different father, Robbie came along. She told me plans were in place for someone to adopt him without her consent, but she stopped it from happening when she found out. Four years later, to another man, she fell pregnant then gave birth to Warren in July 1974. Finally, on 30th December 1976 at Brighton Hospital in Melbourne's South East, I was born. Mum always said she kept trying until she had a girl. I recently found out that Mum would leave for the day, not long after I was born, saying she'd had enough. She would call a sister to come and look after me. When Mum returned, she would yell at whoever was looking after me, telling them to, "Get the fuck out of her house."

Growing up, I thought my mum was beautiful, intelligent, and strong. I admired her, but I knew she was different from my friend's mums. She acted and dressed differently than them. She was younger. She was sexy. She was fun. There were many times I was so proud to be her daughter. I often witnessed her standing up for either herself or us, although how she went about it was not ideal. She would make complaints about products or services – always warranted, mind you – but she never did it with aplomb. There was often yelling, and a scene caused, and as embarrassing as it usually was, I still admired her strength in standing up for what she believed.

There were also times that I wasn't proud. The first time I was embarrassed by something she did was in primary school. I was in grade five or so when Mum came on an excursion with my class. I was so excited. That feeling didn't last long as when I saw what she was wearing, I felt sick. She wore a top that gaped at her chest and was sans bra. I noticed. Others noticed. A boy in my class came over to me and said, "Your mum's not wearing a bra, and we can all see her boobs," in front of everyone. I wanted the earth to open then and there so I could jump in.

When I was in grade four, Mum had an all-expenses-paid trip to Europe via Singapore and Abu Dhabi. One of her wealthy friends paid for the trip. At least, that's what she told me. When she returned, I came home from school excited to see her and found our lounge room floor almost wholly covered in gifts. It was like a thousand Christmases all at once. I still have a few knick-knacks packed away somewhere.

She told us that she went to get her passport while in an airport and found a gold bar stashed in her wallet. She called a friend at home, who organised for her to go to a bank and exchange it for cash. That's how she bought the presents. As a 10-year-old, I believed that. As an adult, I don't.

Family

Growing up, I have such fond memories of spending time with cousins on my mum's side of the family. With 14 cousins, Christmas was one big party. I recall long tables, delicious food, lots of laughs, and finding coins hidden in the pudding. Looking at photos, I feel the happiness from those moments in time.

Being the only girl in my family, I stayed at Aunty Nett's house often, to spend time with her four girls. It was so nice to get away from the testosterone at home. We would sing to Bon Jovi and make up dances, watch Grease on repeat or play elastics in the driveway. It was here that my cousin Jodie comfortably explained what a period was. I wasn't told at home.

I can still smell the bath being run for me at Aunty Judy's house during a visit when I was around four or five. She apologised for only having dinosaurs for me to play with in there. I loved playing with the dogs at Aunty Helen's and remember a game of Monopoly getting out of hand and the board being flipped. Good memories!

We were a close family. Until we weren't. After moving back from Derby, in 1988, we didn't see as much of our family as we used to, and eventually, we didn't see them at all. I never knew why but remember Mum talking negatively about her family. There was always someone who had done something wrong by her. That never changed. One week she would be talking to one sister and the next, she wouldn't. So the cycle went.

It upset me to lose this closeness, particularly with my aunties and female cousins. Thankfully now, through the magic of social media, we are in regular contact. I am so grateful to have that connection again and am thankful for the support I have received, particularly through David's illness and death, and everything since. Aunty Jude, Aunty Nett, cousin Mark, and cousins Jodie, Sue, Jenni, and Shelley, have shown me that I still have family out there, even though my immediate family fell apart years ago.

My siblings

I was 10 or 11 when Mum sat me down in the lounge of our Dingley home and showed me a newspaper article. I was confused when she told me that the girl in the article was my half-sister. My dad had a child before meeting my mum. The report was very distressing. I felt sad for the girl and wondered if I would ever meet her. Over the years, I thought of her often but didn't feel the need to search her out until a few years ago. I have since found out that my parents looked into adopting Cheryl, which would have dramatically changed both of our lives.

A couple of years later, when I was in year seven, Mum told me that Dave and Robbie had different fathers to myself and Warren and that they also had different fathers to each other. (For those finding this hard to follow, I don't blame you, it's complex. Take a look back at the family tree in the preface.) I was shocked, but it didn't change my relationship with them. They were my brothers, regardless. I brought it up with one of my teachers, who helped me understand that all families have skeletons and sometimes hide things for various reasons. After that, I started to see how much of my life was not what it seemed. I could see many lies were beginning to unravel.

Working life

While I was in primary school, Mum worked as a receptionist, or secretary as they were once called, at a couple of different companies. She stopped working when we moved to Derby, and upon returning from living in Western Australia in 1988, Mum began working nights. She told me she was a bookkeeper. Even at 12, I didn't understand why a bookkeeper would work in the evenings. She would take one of those giant red, white and blue striped plastic bags with her every night. One day, when she wasn't home, I opened it only to find lingerie, joints, and condoms. It confirmed my suspicions. I never said anything to her but also never quite looked at her in the same way again.

She worked as a receptionist again for a couple of years, earning $700 per week. In the early 1990s, that was a lot of money. Although she worked during the day and I had visited her workplace, I had my suspicions about why she earned so much.

She then went on to work nights again and continued until around 1995/96. She would sleep odd hours, and I always had to be quiet during the day so that I wouldn't wake her. Then, when I was 15, and it was just the two of us living together in a unit in Noble Park, there was a murder only a few hundred metres from where I slept. I slept with a knife under my mattress from then on, fearing someone would break into our house while I was alone.

Gambling

Mum's gambling started while we lived in that unit in Noble Park. There was a pokies venue around the corner, and she would often spend hours in there, losing all of her money – our rent and groceries money. She had a friend who owned a small grocery store, and we would often go in before it opened and do our shopping for free. This 'friend' also bought her $4,000 diamond earrings that she pawned a few years later. I only found out about that when I asked to wear them at my wedding.

The gambling addiction had set in, and I hate to think about how much she has lost over the years. She had one big win that I know about, of $25,000 in 2007. I suggested I put a chunk of it into an online account for her to go on a holiday the following year, but she declined. It was gone in under two weeks, mostly back into the pokies. However, she did buy me a new pram for which I was very grateful.

With the gambling came lies, so many lies. Years later, my siblings and I would talk to each other about lending money to Mum. We would discover that we had all paid for Christmas lunch one year or had each lent money for the same things. Every cent of it went to the pokies. Mum had manipulated us into not talking about certain things with each other, usually simply by saying don't tell your brother/sister/partner. It was so ingrained in us that we would generally always abide by her requests.

When Mum came home from being out (read that as being at the pokies if you will), if I asked where she had been, she would get defensive and say it was none of my business, or angrily say, "Yes, I was at the pokies, and yes, I lost it all." She would then be in a foul mood for days, and I had to tiptoe around her for fear of making her angry again.

I lived behind a bottle shop in Cheltenham around 1996-98. My housemate was moving out, and my mum suggested she move in.

I didn't have much choice as I couldn't afford to rent independently. I worked as a receptionist and only earned $16,000 a year on a traineeship.

After she moved in, she took over the bills. I was still so naive; I gave her money to take care of it all. As a result, our rent was always overdue, and bills were left unpaid. Many years later, I received a notice from debt collectors about a phone bill from that address. It was in my name, and I had to pay it, plus extra fees. I rang Mum to ask about it, and she yelled and screamed at me. She hated when her lies became unstuck and would always go on the defensive. Even though her own choices caused all her money problems, she would play the victim, yet they affected everyone.

One evening I went out and had forgotten my house keys, which was very unlike me. My friend Scott drove me home, and when I realised Mum was out, I called her. No answer. I called again. No answer. This usually only happened when she was gambling. Scott offered for me to stay at his house, but I declined. The car was open, so I decided to sleep there as Mum shouldn't be too late. After much disagreement, Scott eventually left, and I went to sleep in the back of the wagon, with a spare tyre as a pillow. I awoke in daylight with a stiff neck, and Mum still not home. I called repeatedly, but still no answer. When she finally came home, and I told her what had happened, she yelled at me, blaming me. Sure, I am the one who forgot my keys, but her response was unnecessary and nasty. Again, I had to walk on eggshells.

When we weren't living together, she would often call to ask for money. After I was married, she wouldn't even ask how we were or ask after my kids, she would only call to get money. If I said no, which wasn't often, the call didn't last long. Andrew and I were on a single wage with young kids and didn't have any spare cash. So, whenever I did lend her money, I needed her to pay it back fairly quickly. Every time she borrowed from us, I made that clear, but I would then have terrible arguments with her trying to get it back. When I saw her number come up on the phone, my heart would sink, knowing what would transpire. Every time I got off the phone with her, I would be in a bad mood or simply upset.

Grief

In 1993, my mum's mum passed away. Mum changed after this. She was devastated and cried all the time. Her health deteriorated, and there was always something wrong with her. She had heart conditions, overactive thyroid, underactive thyroid, depression, gynaecological issues, and much more that I don't specifically recall. I only ever remember her being tired or unwell after her mum died.

Understandably, Warren's death utterly broke Mum and she became a shell of her former self. In the year that followed, not much changed. We didn't celebrate much of anything that year, and when Warren's birthday was nearing, I suggested that we all go out for dinner together to honour him. She told me it was a ridiculous idea. Her behaviour became more erratic and hostile as the years went on.

A couple of years later, our family was having a meeting with a police officer to help us understand the outcome of Warren's court case. Mum asked after a particular officer who led the case. The officer told us he had since died of cancer. After saying she was happy that he had died due to how he treated our family before and after the court case, the officer shut her down. The man they were talking about had been his friend. She stormed off in a rage and wouldn't come back inside until the officer left. We apologised to him and thanked him for coming. Regardless of the actions and behaviour of the officer leading the case, what Mum said was horrible, and I was ashamed and embarrassed.

We were all devastated after Warren died and grieved in our own ways. Our family fell apart, rather than becoming closer because of the tragedy, and we were never the same unit again. Still dysfunctional, but worse.

Suicide

Around 1998/99, on Grand Final Day, I was at a friend's annual BBQ. I loved going to this annual event. All my closest friends were there, as well as their parents. It was always a great day, full of laughs and a game of street footy at halftime. Not long after I arrived, I received a call from Robbie. He said Mum had called Joanne, his partner, and said goodbye. Straight away, we knew what that meant. Mum had often talked about not having any reason to stick around. She had threatened it so many times that I would always be careful not to do anything to upset her.

After the call, I was crying and told my friends I had to leave, not knowing what lay ahead. I drove from Moorabbin to Robbie's house in Cranbourne, around 30kms, and Robbie and I then went to Mum's house in Hastings, checking car parks for her car at pokies venues along the way. When we arrived at her home, a note was on the door saying, "I'm out the back, don't come around. Call the police." Of course, the first thing we did was rush around the back. We found her unconscious in the front seat of her car with the hose running from the exhaust and through the nearly closed window. Robbie opened the door, turned the car off, and dragged her body out, cutting her ankle on the door frame as her limp body was pulled down to the grass. He told me to call an ambulance and wait out front for it. I did that, crying the whole time.

Although time stood still at that moment, the ambulance was quick to arrive and took her to the hospital. Robbie and I drove there, meeting Dave once we arrived. While the doctors worked on her, we stood out front together in shock. When we walked back in, there was a commotion. Mum was angry that she was alive and wanted to leave immediately. However, the doctors wanted her to stay overnight for observation and a psych evaluation. So, being the ever-obedient kids, we smuggled her out with security on our tail. In the core of my being, I knew we were doing the wrong thing, but going against something Mum asked us to do seemed the better of two evils.

When we arrived back at her house, there were notes on the kitchen bench, one for each of us. She wouldn't let me read mine but eventually gave in. It didn't say much of anything. I remember thinking, that's it? That's all you wanted to leave for me? I felt so selfish thinking that, but at the same time, I was honestly so disappointed and felt I didn't mean enough to her to write more. I stayed with her that night and was glad when the police visited to check on her well-being. She was defensive and rude to them, saying she didn't need help. I just stood back, too scared to say what I felt. I wanted to yell, "Take her away!" I woke many times to check on her, making sure she was breathing and hadn't tried to kill herself while I was asleep.

The following day, she brought in the hose she used and showed me the kink in it, flippantly saying, "That's why it didn't work." To my knowledge, she never sought professional help after this. She later told me that she had tried a few years earlier and was found on a beach on Phillip Island by strangers. She had overdosed on pills. I didn't speak of it again, fearing it would upset her and that she would try again.

I was home with the kids when Andrew came home early from work one day around 2009/10. Immediately, I knew something was wrong. He told me Dave had called him at work to tell him that Mum had attempted suicide again. This time she took pills, poured petrol around the unit she was living in, lit it, then wrapped herself in wet towels and lay on the couch to die. Before doing so, though, in a clear cry for help, she called Robbie, who was working in Perth, saying goodbye. Robbie rang Joanne, who called Dave. Both Joanne and Dave went over to try and save her. Dave broke into the unit, made his way through the thick smoke, and dragged her out. He scooped black ash from her throat and gave her mouth to mouth until the ambulance arrived. She survived and was angry when she woke.

I can't help but wonder if the smoke that Dave inhaled that day had anything to do with his cancer.

My wedding

When I became engaged, Mum was excited and looked forward to my wedding. She had a beautiful dress made but couldn't afford to pick it up once complete, so I paid for it. Who knows, my siblings possibly did too! I wanted Dave and Robbie to walk me partway down the aisle and for Mum to walk me the rest. It was not traditional, but neither was our family. On the morning of my wedding, she arrived late, putting me on edge. We planned to go to a cafe for breakfast and then head to the Westin Hotel in Melbourne, where we would get ready for the big day. The rest of the morning went well until it was time for the photos. Again, untraditionally, we had our pictures taken before the ceremony. It was a brisk September day, and Mum was cold. She borrowed the groomsman's jacket and ruined the expensive corsage we bought for her. I found out later that she told our photographer what a bitch I was for getting upset.

My kids

Before my first anniversary with Andrew, our first son Connor was born. In the very early days, Mum would come over to visit, but only when I could pay for her petrol. She would sit at the table and do crosswords or have a coffee. I had hoped for some help but was too tired to ask and didn't want to upset her. I knew it would end in an argument if I said anything.

After a tough night, she visited, and we were talking. I opened up about how hard I was finding life as a first-time parent, and she went on to say how hard her life is and that she is only around because of her first-born grandchild. Talk about a knife to the heart. She only ever had Connor overnight once. I honestly didn't trust her. She would smoke in the house and have painkillers often, so I could never honestly believe she wouldn't do those things while he was there. She loved seeing the kids, but it was never quite what I imagined their relationship to be like.

Estrangement

In 2008, after more of the same lies, more of the borrowed money, and more constant negativity, it all came to a head on Christmas day. I had asked Mum not to shower the kids with the ridiculous amount of gifts like she had always done and preferred her to spend the money on petrol to come and see them instead. She promised she wouldn't go overboard, but when we turned up, we saw the mountain of gifts piled up against the wall. There were at least 10 gifts per grandchild, and there were 10 grandchildren.

I was terribly unwell with a chest infection and was also tired, having two toddlers. I sat in the corner while she gave out presents, sometimes even throwing them to the recipient. I was frustrated and disappointed that she had not done what I asked, yet she seemed pretty proud of herself. Mum gave all of the kids so many presents – mostly crappy toys that they wouldn't use – that they barely had time to look at each present before she threw the next their way. Mum had a look she would give, and I saw it this day. It felt like she knew she had done the wrong thing and had gotten away with it but didn't care. There was a smugness to the look like she had won.

Later, she was offering ice cream to all the kids. I said Connor couldn't have any as he hadn't eaten any of his Christmas lunch. He was three at the time, and even though it was Christmas day, I was consistent with my discipline. Finally, we were in the kitchen, and she had the fridge door open. She looked over the door and, with pure hatred in her eyes, said, "Your kids are going to grow up to hate you." That was the final straw. I lost it. I yelled back, saying I was sick of her telling me how to parent. I said a whole lot more but can't remember any of it. I was so hurt; the rest of the encounter is a blur. I was crying, struggling to breathe, and told Andrew we had to leave. We gathered up the kids, with our eldest screaming because he didn't want to go, packed everything in the car with Dave's help, and left.

To many, this singular incident seems innocuous. But, to me, it was a lifetime of hurt, frustration, anger, and sadness, all pouring out of me. The fact that Mum always blatantly did whatever would suit her, regardless of how it affected anyone else, had run its course, and I had finally had enough. As much as it hurt, I decided that this was the end of our relationship in that split second. I was no longer going to put up with the lies, the narcissistic behaviour, and the feeling that I was never good enough. I was certainly not going to let her drag my kids into that cycle. Five days later, on my birthday, I got a text message to say happy birthday and to call her when we returned from our holiday. I responded with 'thank you' but didn't call when I returned. I haven't seen her since that day. I hadn't spoken to her either until my recent phone call to discuss the DNA results.

> Children of narcissists are often highly intuitive. They know when something secret is going on in their family. They may not be able to put their finger exactly on it and it usually takes time for the exact truth to form but by keen observation, eventually they know the truth. Children of narcissists are often truth seekers. They are among the most empathetic of individuals.
>
> - Dr Linda Martinez-Lewi

REFLECTIONS

I often offered to help Mum become healthier, reduce all her medications, and seek alternative ways to treat her myriad of illnesses. But, unfortunately, I believe she never wanted to get better and relished playing the victim. In the 32 years with Mum in my life, there were only around seven or so that seemed 'normal' to me. When she was in the right frame of mind, she was a fantastic mum. She was thoughtful and generous, fun and loving. When she wasn't, she was tough to be around.

It's difficult grieving a person who is still living, but that is what I have done. I mourn the relationship we should have had, and I feel sad that my kids have grown up without their Nanny. I know that I have done the right thing for both myself and my family, but there isn't a day that goes by that I don't miss the 'good' mum. I am saddened that my mum is never going to be the mum I need her to be.

It wasn't until I ceased the relationship with my mum that I could gain clarity. I now realise she has a narcissistic personality, and I have done many hours of research to heal and understand how this affects people. I never understood why I always felt like I was wrong and why I always wanted to do the right thing by her. Of course, most kids want to do right by their parents, but I felt that all hell would break loose if I did the wrong thing. I never realised that her behaviour made me feel like I was the crazy one; like everything was my fault. With the knowledge I have now, I have freed myself from any guilt or shame that I have carried over the years. Narcissists gaslight and make you question your own beliefs, and I now know that none of this was ever my fault.

Mum always went to incredible lengths for my costumes, hand-making many of them.

Left: Me, dressed up in 1980/81, in my costume made out of crepe paper. Middle: Mum made my award-winning Easter bonnet, 1980. Right: Me dressed up as Cyndi Lauper, around 1986.

Mum and me on my wedding day.

Andrew and Connor in front of the mountain of Christmas presents, 2008.

Cousins Jacinta, Jenni, Susan, Aunty Judy and me in 2015.

Chapter 3

Home Sweet Home(less)

The noise of packing tape screeching across a box is the sound of my nightmares. Piles of flattened cardboard boxes, bubble wrap, newspapers, and sharpies. The blood from cutting your knuckles in a doorway as you carry another heavy box. Bruises on your thighs from boxes leaning on you as you pick them up to put them in another stack. The sweat dripping from your dust-covered body on moving day. Pure exhaustion after cleaning yet another rental before you can move in. Telling your children you have to move, again...

I was never quite homeless, but I knew what eviction meant from an early age. Living in rented homes all my life was normal to me. I never felt secure or settled, always knowing we would be moving again at some stage. When you Google the most stressful events in a person's life, moving house is in the top five. I am currently living in my 38th house. Yes, 38! I can pack a box like no one you've ever met but have carried the stress of moving house all my life.

I had lived in at least 10 homes before finishing high school. My friends came to know never to write my address and phone number in pen. I have lived in Noble Park, Endeavour Hills, Dingley, Cheltenham, Moorabbin, Derby (WA), Hastings, Murrumbeena, Oakleigh East, Mount Waverley, and Ashwood. The majority of places I have lived in three, four, or five different times. I have lived in a caravan in suburbia, stayed in a hotel, slept on the floor of a friend's room in a house she was boarding in, stayed in a women's shelter, moved in with a boyfriend's family, lived with a brother and his family, rented a unit behind a bottle shop, as well as various houses, units, and apartments. Six years is the longest I have been in one home, and I recently moved four times in just two years. As a tenant, you are at the mercy of the landlord, although Victorian laws are now changing to be fairer for renters.

Ironically, as I am writing this, the landlord of the property I currently live in has notified me that he is selling. I have been here two years and still have another year on my lease. If an investor buys, I can stay. If it's someone who wants to move in, I can't. So I remain optimistic that I won't need to pack more boxes over the next year.

The idea of change was great in my early 20s, but now as a mother, the stress of not knowing if the owner will renew my lease hangs over me. In addition, the cost of renting has skyrocketed in the last decade. For example, when I first became engaged in 2002, we paid $265 per week for a three-bedroom home in Oakleigh East. Now, in 2021, I am paying $680 per week for a three-bedroom house in Ashwood. Granted, it does have a pool and a fantastic studio where I work, but on a single wage, it's damn hard.

Every move meant a substantial rent increase, along with the $5000 plus it costs to move home and office. When you combine all the connections and disconnections, packing materials, take away food when you're too tired to cook, the moving van or removalists, the list is almost endless. And don't get me started on furniture. We always had mismatched hand-me-downs and pieces we bought to suit a particular house, only to find it didn't fit the next home. In addition, the kids have had multiple beds due to varying bedroom sizes in the rentals.

The financial cost is just one facet of this stress-inducing task. Being a business owner, I went without pay when I took time off and juggled work around the move. As a result, I would be exhausted in the weeks leading up to the house move, and the weeks after, due to packing, cleaning, unpacking, and more cleaning. The physical exertion of moving is beyond any tiredness I have ever felt, even as the mother of a child who didn't sleep through the night until he was three.

Every home I have rented has been left cleaner than when I moved in, which perhaps doesn't say much, as every house I have moved into was filthy. The legal term of reasonably clean is such a grey area. I can assure you that my version of reasonable is not the same as the previous tenants. I don't keep a spotlessly clean home, but I expect the home I move into to be clean. When I moved into the house I am currently in, I rang the real estate and demanded a cleaner come the same day to clean it. Imagine spinifex rolling through a ghost town. This house had dog fur rolling through the lounge, the kitchen, even the oven. We also found chewed gum in the bathroom drawer. On top of that, the condition report took over two hours to complete as the real estate agent didn't bother providing an accurate one. When leaving a previously rented property, the real estate agent called and requested me to go back and patch a tiny dint in a wall that was the size of a 10c piece. I knew that was there when we moved in but had not written it on the report. Rookie! So, on a 40-degree day, with two toddlers in tow, I went to Bunnings, bought my supplies, went back to the house, and patched the wall.

That same house was my nightmare house. Besides being disgustingly filthy when we moved in, we dealt with a flooding dishwasher and washing machine tap, disintegrating decking, malfunctioning heating, a gas leak, and ducted heating full of dry cat food, amongst many other things. We only stayed there for 11 months, and I took the landlord to the Victorian Civil and Administration Tribunal twice during that time. I won the cases, but the toll it took on my mental health was not worth it. Preparing for a court case, sitting for an entire day in the waiting room only for the case to be adjourned, and the nerves when having to speak to the judge are just some of the things that caused me stress during this time. The emotions were pouring out of me during the hearing. It all contributed to terrible anxiety that I still deal with some ten years on.

After moving into a new rental, there is always a month or two when you find all the things that don't work or are broken, that you can never know in the 10-to-15-minute inspection you are initially granted. Then, there's paperwork to fill out and appointments with tradies to organise. I am fortunate to work from home and can accommodate these disruptions, but the time spent is forever lost on something somebody should have tended to before we moved in.

I hope to one day own a house and finally feel the security that bricks and mortar can bring. Then, I want to paint a wall, renovate, and plant roots. One slight positive in moving homes so often is the pleasant surprise I get when springtime comes and the garden blooms.

REFLECTIONS

I had never known the feeling of community, not until my children started primary school, and to not provide a stable home for them has broken my heart repeatedly. As I am currently watching them get anxious and stressed about the possibility of another house move, all I can hope is that if we do have to move, I can find a suitable home for my kids and something that can function as a workplace and studio.

To help ease the discomfort of moving, Andrew and I always tried to involve the kids in the house hunting and choice of bedrooms. We would explore our new local areas and make our move like an adventure for them. We would always make an effort to create exciting bedrooms, sometimes separate toy rooms. Although we never owned the houses we moved into, we always made them a home. And that's just it, if my kids are happy and settled, it doesn't matter where we are, as long as we have a roof over our head.

I have had many people look down at me over the years for not owning my home. There have been snide comments, ignorant questions, and looks of pity. Many years ago, a dear friend's mum told me a story of one of her friends, who also rents, and how she loves the freedom of being able to move whenever she wants. She told me there is no shame in renting and that chat has stayed with me over the years, helping to ease my mind when I deal with people who don't understand my situation.

Me in the front yard of our house in Endeavour Hills, around 1978.

Me posing near the front door of our house in Dingley, around 1985.

In the front yard of our house in Derby, Western Australia in 1988.

My home at the back of a bottle shop, 1997.

Life is like riding a bicycle.
To keep your balance, you must keep moving.

– Albert Einstein

The house in Oakleigh East that Andrew and I first moved into together, and where we lived when our children were born.

Top: The nightmare house in Mount Waverley, 2009.

Left: We lived in this house in Mount Waverley in 2018. We signed a two-year lease but had to move after only nine months when the owner had to sell.

Chapter 4

The New Kid in School

My first memories of school were at Chalcot Lodge Kindergarten in Endeavour Hills. I remember the smell of fruit time, with cut-up oranges and apples, and fondly look back on the professional photos taken of the little blonde girl in the playground and standing at an easel.

I went on to Mossgiel Park Primary School, also in Endeavour Hills. I loved going to the same school as my big brother Warren and was so proud to see the logo my mum designed on the uniforms, which is still in use today. I met my first best friend here – Emma. We were inseparable. I loved going to her house, full of the noise of multiple siblings. When she moved to the country, I visited and remembered chasing bunnies through the yard, collecting mail at the end of the long driveway, and a newborn calf suckling on my arm.

At the end of grade one, we moved, and I started at Kingswood Primary School in Dingley at the beginning of the new school year. Four people bullied me at this school, two boys and two girls. Three were in the same year level, and one was the older sister of the girl who bullied me. I was taunted, called names, and hit. I would pick fights with one of the boys who bullied me, in an attempt to show him he didn't scare me, and ended up in the principal's office after kicking him in the crown jewels. The other boy would ruin my lunch almost daily. Thankfully, I met and became friends with Bee. I adored her, thought her parents were the loveliest people I had ever met and idolised her big sister. I spent so much time at their house I should have paid rent. After-school fun and weekend sleepovers were constant. I loved going to her parent's bedroom to call my mum on their green push-button phone to see if I could stay the night. We would jump on the trampoline, play in their pool and ride through the streets. The squeaky fold-out bed gave me the feeling of belonging, and I felt so safe there. Bee and I are still friends today, 37 years later.

Grade six brought about change again when we moved to Derby in May. I was so upset about leaving my friends and was daunted at the thought of going to school in a new state. Western Australia didn't have a prep class, so I went into year seven. Here I was, this short, skinny, Melbournian, now in a classroom that was half-filled with Aboriginal children. It was an extraordinary experience for me. I had never seen an Aboriginal person before. Some of the girls were quite tall and would stare me down. I was frightened but so intrigued by the way they behaved in class. They were allowed to get up and leave the classroom any time they liked, constantly disrupting the class. The only thing I remember learning at the school was a beautiful new way to write in a fancy cursive script. We spent breaks playing games like dodging the shadows of the kites flying above us. They came out in force when food was around, and I was frightened by them, particularly after the little adventure Warren and I had on the mudflats near home.

School here started and finished earlier than in Melbourne due to the heat. After school most days, Warren and I would go to the pool, as did most other students. It was always great fun and an excellent way to cool off before heading home each day. We spent a lot of time wandering the airport and surrounding areas. A highlight of living this close to the airport was meeting Bob Hawke, the then prime minister of Australia, when he flew in. He was charming and seemed genuinely interested in talking to us. We then went on a school excursion to the local RAAF base to see him speak. I felt so important, having already met him.

Another Australian icon we met in this tiny town was Dick Smith. On our way to the local Chinese restaurant one evening, we decided to go to the pier to see the sunset when we heard a commotion.

A teenage boy was throwing live bats, found under the dock, up to the kites flying above. The kites were extraordinary, diving down to catch their dinner. Dick Smith's daughter disagreed and was yelling at the boy to stop. He did eventually but wasn't happy about it. Dick came over to lead his daughter away but did stop to say hello to us.

After only a few months, we were on the move again, staying in Perth for a couple of weeks before returning to Melbourne. Back in Melbourne, Warren, Mum, and I shared a bedroom at an aunt's unit until we found somewhere to live. We settled not far from that unit in Cheltenham, and I started at Kingston Heath Primary School in August. Being my third school in one year, I missed my grade six class photo. My teacher was a proper, older woman who dressed immaculately and had the most beautiful nails I'd ever seen. One of my other teachers was the husband of one of my teachers from Kingswood Primary School. He was just as lovely as his wife. I felt comfortable here. No one bullied me, no one called me names, and I met Susan (Sue), who would become my new best friend.

Like Bee, Sue and I spent a lot of time together. We would walk the streets talking for hours, go and watch the baseball at Waverley Park (go Reds!), play pool at Fast Eddies, and shared our deepest secrets. I smoked my first joint with Sue. We were on a hill in a park near her house, and I remember us in fits of laughter in front of a mirror shop, looking at our stoned reflections. We remained friends when we started year seven at different schools, and eventually, Sue changed schools and came to the same one as me.

Orientation day at Cheltenham Secondary College saw me reconnect with friends from Kingswood Primary School and meet new friends. There were many ups and downs during high school, and like any teen, there was plenty of angst. Schoolyard crushes, bullies, rumours, and depression filled my years here. In my younger years, I was stabbed with pins and pushed around on the school bus. One instance included my watch being smashed. I had a teacher embarrass me in front of the class in year 10, which ended in me swearing at him and walking out of the classroom. Yet, looking back, I remember it as one of the happiest times of my life. I had incredible friends, fantastic art teachers who took me under their wings, and I built a resilience I didn't know I was capable of having.

This school is where I came into my own as a creative. I was the first year 10 student ever invited to join the year 12 life drawing class and created the yearbook cover when I was in year 12 as one of my assessment tasks. In year 10, I also began a part-time course at Photography Studies College. Every Wednesday after school, I would catch a bus to the train station and then the train into the city, where I would change out of my uniform in the Flinders Street Station public toilets. I would then head across the Yarra River to attend a three-hour adult photography class in Southbank. I felt completely overwhelmed and like a fraud. I didn't fit in and honestly thought the other students laughed at me behind my back, and the teachers rolled their eyes when I spoke. My saving grace was meeting Joe, who went on to run a successful photography business and was the photographer at my wedding. I have plans to visit him soon to discuss a business collaboration.

Although I moved house several times to many different suburbs during high school, I asked to remain at the same school. Unfortunately, it meant 5.30 am alarms to catch two buses to school, leaving in the dark and returning home in the dark. I am eternally grateful that I was strong enough to remain at this school, purely because of the friendships I made. My friends have supported me through the most challenging times in my life and laughed with me through the funniest. We have watched each other grow up, find love, marry and have children, though not always in that order. They make me feel like the luckiest person to know them.

I have had to lean on these friends so often – financially, physically, and emotionally. I am sure they roll their eyes when I announce I have to move house yet again but always offer support before, during, or after. They have held me through my grief, and when I had to move house a couple of months after Dave died, my army stepped up and helped with car load after car load, as well as with packing and cleaning. They know I appreciated all they have done for me, but I don't think they realise how many times their support has brought me back from the brink. I took a moment during that particular move to step back and watch for a minute. The gratitude I felt filled me that day and gave me the energy to keep going.

During one of these moves, my friend Greg was carrying out my computer, which had gone to Apple heaven. I said, "I don't even know why I'm taking that with me; it's dead." The next day, Greg rang and offered to lend me however much I needed to buy a new computer, as well as the software to go with it. I burst into tears. That generous offer allowed me to start my graphic design business that is still going strong, a decade later. It wasn't much to him, but it meant more to me than I can say.

Although I don't see my high school crew as often as I used to, I know that when we do, it fills my cup until the next time, and I can't wait to make many more memories with them.

Me at Chalcot Lodge Kindergarten.

REFLECTIONS

Education is obviously important but it's the friends and memories created that made my time at school bearable.

Having to change primary school so often in grade six was unsettling. Not only was my home life a mess that year, moving so much, and missing many weeks of school made my last year of primary school extremely difficult. Having to fit in built resilience. It enabled me to see a strength within me, but in saying that, I was vulnerable going into high school.

I knew many kids at Cheltenham Secondary already, but they were from different schools and I had to find a way to find my people. It's not unlike most kids going into year seven, but I felt I was carrying a lot more baggage than most and just wanted to focus on friendships, art, and learning.

The bullying I received in high school made me stronger on the outside, but on the inside, I was hurting. I would show up every day, but it was a struggle. Every time I stepped onto the school bus, both before and after school, I wondered what horror would await me. I couldn't tell my mum about it because I knew she would overreact and cause a scene that would make my school life even more difficult.

I am now the mother of two high school boys and often reflect on what I went through, and hope they aren't going through anything similar. It's hard to tell with teens, especially boys! I hope every day that I am supporting them enough, so they can get through these difficult years unscathed.

My first day of Prep.

My first day of high school.

Year 12.

Graduation day for my Associate Diploma of Arts – Design course.

Top: Bee and me, around 1986.

Left: Me and Bee at her sister's wedding, around 2003.

Below: Sue and me, around 1990.

Bottom: Sue and me before our year 10 formal.

Top: Jodie and me when we had an overnight adventure in the city with Mum, around 1990.

Left: Jodie and me on my wedding day, 2004.

Below: I'm not drunk, you're drunk! Jodie and me at Susie's 40th birthday.

Bottom: Jodie and me, around 1998.

Above: Ben and me at Greg's 18th, 1994.
Right: Ben and me at Brooke's 40th, 2016.

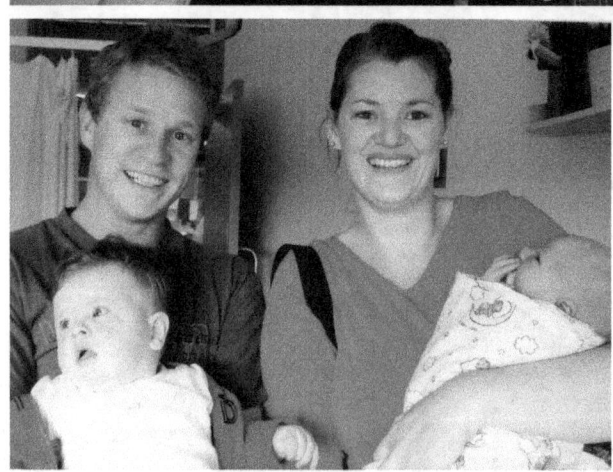

Above: Scott and me at a 16th birthday, around 1991.

Left: Scott, holding Connor, and me, holding Scott's newborn son, 2006.

Greg and me at Scott's sister's 21st, 1999.

Scott, Greg, me, and Ben at Greg and Karen's wedding, 2003.

Baz and me at our year 10 formal, 1992.

Scott, Greg, Baz, Ben, and me, hugging after my 21st speech, 1997.

Baz and me at my 21st, 1997.

Left: Brooke (Boozmato) and me at my 21st, 1997.

Above: Brooke and me at Ben and Susie's wedding in Bali, 2004.

Below: Me and Susie at Brooke's 40th, 2004.

Above: Karen, Jodie, and me at Ben and Susie's wedding in Bali, 2004.

Right: Susie, me, and Peta at Scott's sister's 21st, 1999.

Below: Peta, Brooke, Jodie, Karen, and me at my hen's day/night, 2004.

Me and Kate on a camping trip in Bright, 2002.

Kate and me at a 1970s fancy dress, 2018.

Brooke, Greg, Baz, Scott, and me (front), Ben taking a specky (back), at Baz's 40th, 2016.

The Gang: Me, Peta, Jodie, Baz, Brooke, and Greg (front), Scott and Ben (back), at Kinga's Krazy Kids Kris Kringle, 2019. Thirty years of friendship right here, and even more for Scott, Greg and Ben.

> In the end you always go back to the people that were there in the beginning.
>
> **– Unknown**

Chapter 5

Sex(uality)

Sex and sexuality played a significant role in my upbringing. I would watch Mum get dressed up to go out, wearing clothes to show off her beautiful body. I thought that's what women had to do to get attention. Her make-up would be immaculate, accentuating her striking features. Men often looked her way when we were out. On my wedding day, after we were both dressed and made up, she walked me through the hallway of the Westin Hotel to see my future husband, Andrew, for the first time that day. A stranger stopped us and inappropriately asked for her number.

As a four- or five-year-old, Mum taught me a dance, which was so much fun. As I got older, I realised the dance was quite sexy, and the music wouldn't be out of place in a strip club. Other music played in the home was not quite suitable for kids, such as *I Wonder* by Rodriguez. I would happily sing along, not understanding the lyrics, "I wonder how many times you had sex, I wonder do you know who'll be next."

Mum would also put make-up on me and then take photos. Looking back on these photos I now question why she did it as I look more like an adult than a child in them. Perhaps it was just mother-daughter time. Photos aside, I was allowed to wear make-up from around

13 to 14 years old. Even without make-up, I always looked older than my years. As a teen, people often mistook me for a university student. I'm sure my height helped. I am 175cm and was 14 when I reached that height.

I was allowed to wear whatever I wanted, and Mum happily bought me clothes that weren't necessarily suitable for my age. I loved being able to express myself through clothing when I was younger, as many teen girls do, and I liked the way boys would notice me. I never dressed in something that left nothing to the imagination, but I knew what clothes worked for my maturing body.

Due to Mum's love of photography and art, there were books of nudes on hand in our home. I was fascinated by them, and there were two that I easily recall. The photos in the first book were of women – some fully naked, some half-naked, and some touching each other. I thought they were so beautiful. The soft focus and lacy lingerie intensified the eroticism for me. I would look at this book far more often than my mum probably knew. The other book was big and heavy and was full of erotic drawings and art. They depicted self-love, orgies, lesbianism, and traditional sex, from ancient, oriental art through to modern. As I matured, this book excited me more as I knew I wanted to experience some of the scenes I saw.

On my 16th birthday, Mum gave me Madonna's *Sex* book, for the photographic art of course! It was basically porn, with images depicting lesbianism, scenes of rape, and everything in between. Erotic text also filled the pages. I was pretty young when I first saw porn. Having older brothers had a lot to do with that. I would walk into their bedroom and see magazines or even see it playing on their TV. At 13, one brother even had a pornographic game on the computer that he would play in front of me.

Early on, I knew I was attracted to both men and women but was never comfortable talking to anyone about it. It was not something you talk about in the schoolyard at the age of 13 or 14. As I matured, I felt I could talk to friends about it. Now, I am very comfortable in my skin, and it doesn't bother me who knows. I am living my authentic life. Being creative, I was interested in art from an early age and often saw nudity in paintings or photographs. I was always drawn to the female figure, finding it far more beautiful to look at than a male body. I frequently drew females, focusing on their curves.

During my high school orientation, I was embarrassed but somewhat excited when a girl came up to me and told me, "That boy over there likes you." A couple of years later, I kissed that boy on a beach at a friend's birthday party, and we had an on-again/off-again relationship throughout high school. He was one of many through high school – some from school and others not – and I was often called a slut. Apparently, kissing multiple boys was frowned upon. I knew I wasn't a slut, but I did enjoy kissing different people and didn't understand why others thought it was wrong.

I lost my virginity to a man when I was 16. He was 22. He was a friend of my brothers, and we 'went out' for around 10 months. I always felt older than my years, so it seemed natural to date older men. In my heart of hearts, I knew it wouldn't last because of our age difference, but we are still friends and keep in contact online, with the occasional in-person catch-up. However, the majority of my boyfriends were older, with the most significant age gap being 11 years when I was 20. One boyfriend, who was one of the few my own age, was allowed to sleep over, in my bed. I was also allowed to sleep at his house. We were 16 at the time. A year later, I moved in with that boyfriend and his family after being evicted from our home.

Looking back on these relationships, I always looked for the father figure I never had. On the one hand, I wanted someone to look after me the way my father never did. On the other, I knew someone older would understand me better than someone my age. I matured mentally at a young age and often felt out of place around people my age.

I first kissed a girl when I was 18 or 19 and lost my 'virginity' to a girl when I was 20. It was a girl from school who followed me home after a party. I know it sounds a bit stalkerish, but I was so flattered and remembered the nervousness of that first real encounter. I experimented over the following years until I met my husband. Now, as a single woman, I have experimented some more but know I would prefer a man as a partner over a woman.

During my early 20s, I went out every weekend and usually met someone different each time. I enjoyed discovering someone new, and although I wanted to settle down, I also wanted to experience life. I met people in clubs, at work, and even got a phone number while stopped at a red light. I ended up meeting the 'red light guy' at the Espy for a drink, and again, at his house. These were only ever hook-ups, always casual, and I knew I wouldn't meet the love of my life that way, but it was a lot of fun trying.

I met a well-spoken man who was also a few years older than me on a night out for my ex-boyfriend's birthday. I was 18, and he was 24. We met at a club where he was working, and I asked for his number and called the next day. He came to meet me properly a few days later. I was so embarrassed as I was living in a caravan at the time, but thankfully, that didn't faze him. We met only a few times before he told me he was moving to Canada. He came to my TAFE during my lunch break, pulled out his guitar, and sang a song he'd written for me. It was beautiful. He then said if I weren't 18, he'd ask me to marry him and go to Canada with him. Wait, what? I didn't see him again.

Another man I had a fleeting fling with was from Croatia. I've always had a thing for men from other countries. Unsurprisingly, I also met him at a club. We had passed each other a few times and given each other the once over. Unfortunately, I had to leave and couldn't find him to give him my number. As I neared the door to exit, there he was. I whispered in his ear that I wanted his number. Unfortunately, I didn't have my phone or a pen and had to remember it. I got in the taxi with my friends and said the number out loud over and over again. The next day, with a massive hangover, I called. We talked for two hours before meeting the following week. We had an incredibly intense first kiss across his kitchen counter. If I still remember it clearly some 20 years on, it must have been quite the kiss! Again, we saw each other a couple of times before moving on.

I did have a couple of long relationships, of a year or two, during the years before I met my husband. Andrew and I were together for 18 years and married for 15.

I wasn't the only LGBTQ+ member in my family. With all the photography books and a t-shirt emblazoned with 'Dip me in honey and throw me to the lesbians,' I only have assumptions when it comes to my mum. Warren had one long-term girlfriend before he came out. He never actually said the words to me, but I innately knew and was told by Dave.

During one of my 'homeless' stages, I lived on the bedroom floor of a friend who was boarding in one of her friend's houses. I needed to get out and went to a nearby phone box to call Dave. I knew I couldn't live with Mum and honestly can't remember where she was living at the time. On the phone, Dave said I could move in with him, his partner, and their toddler daughter and came straight to pick me up. Not long after we started driving, he mentioned that he saw a lot of our brother Warren. I thought it was odd that Dave would say that. Of course he did. I knew they were close. He then said, "There's something I need to tell you about Warren." I said, "What? That he's gay?" Dave turned to me, shocked, and said, "How did you know?" I had always just known. I don't know how else to explain it. Dave told me that Mum thought it best that I didn't know yet. For what reason, I will never know. I am a very open-minded person, and Mum thought she needed to 'protect me' from that knowledge... It still astounds me to this day. Warren went on to have a partner until he died.

> I think choosing between men and women
> is like choosing between cake and ice cream.
> You'd be daft not to try both when there are
> so many different flavours.
>
> – Björk

REFLECTIONS

I have never understood the way women are frowned upon for displaying their sexuality or why it's OK for men to have multiple partners but not women. The norm never really suited me, and my honesty and forthrightness have sometimes got me on the wrong side of people. It made me realise that they simply weren't my people. My people don't judge me and have only ever said, "Be careful." I believe sexuality is not something to be hidden away behind closed doors. Sure, there's a time and a place for discussions and displays, but it's a part of being human. Physical contact with another person can be one of the most satisfying, pleasurable, and enlightening experiences. There is no place in my life for judging someone's wants and needs if they are different from my own.

I have been on an exciting journey for the last year, meeting people who I usually perhaps wouldn't have met. I have had some wonderful experiences and met some charming people. I have also met or connected with a whole lotta interesting people. Stay tuned for another book!

Me at approximately seven years of age.

Me aged five.

Me at approximately six years of age.

Dressed up for my year 10 formal, aged 15.

Before my year 12 formal, wearing a suit, aged 16.

Me, aged 10.

Chapter 6

He Ain't Heavy

Warren was a quiet child who grew into a gentle and introverted man. He loved cars, starting with a massive matchbox collection, through to his wheel cap collection. Warren was never a studious kid and left school on his 15th birthday. He only held menial jobs without any qualifications, like removals, forklift driving, and factory hand.

I always thought there was something about Warren that seemed like he was hiding something. I would later find out that it was his sexuality. We never discussed it, but I thought he was ashamed. I didn't care, he was my brother, and as long as he was happy, I was happy. It didn't change the way I felt about him. If anything, it made his life make more sense to me.

On 28th November 1997, I was at work in Moorabbin when I saw Robbie drive into the car park. My first thought was, 'what has Mum done now?' Little did I know that my world was about to fall apart. I walked to the door and let him in, and he walked to the couch in the foyer where we sat down. He didn't mince his words and simply said, "Warren was in a car accident last night. He was killed." He then held me in a firm embrace as I broke down. A colleague walked in during this, saw I was upset, and soon my boss came in to check on me. She asked what had happened, and Robbie said, "Her brother was killed last night." She collected my belongings, and Robbie and I left.

On our way to Robbie's house, I rang my housemate Sue, who knew Warren well. She had been staying with her mum after a knee reconstruction. When I told her what had happened, she fell to the floor. The rest of the trip was a blur. When we arrived, Mum was out front, a broken soul. We hugged and cried and went back inside. As the day progressed, we learned more about the accident. Warren was driving through a green light from Army Road onto Princes Highway in Pakenham when a B Double truck ran a red light and hit his car. His car spun numerous times before stopping on the other side of the highway, many metres from the intersection. The coroner said he died on impact. Further details came out during the court case, which I will discuss later. During the day, one of my aunties called the local police to find out where Warren's body was. Without covering the receiver, the officer yelled out to someone in the background, "Who was on beef duty last night?" Un-fucking-believable.

My memory is a little fuzzy on the exact happenings for the rest of that day. I was in turmoil, my head throbbed from endless tears, and I was sunburnt from sitting outside too long. I told Mum I was supposed to have my work Christmas party that night, that I had organised, and she told me to go. She said it would be good to be around friends for support. I did end up going, and it was surreal, like an out-of-body experience, and it was awful. I did get a lot of support but also had a strange interaction with the business owner. He came over to my table with a smile on his face, and said, "What happened?" It was like he was asking about something happy or fun, not about the death of my brother. I looked at him with disdain and flatly stated, "A truck went through a red light and killed my brother." I couldn't wait to get out of there. Who were these people, and why the hell was I there?

I don't recall if it was the Friday or Saturday after the accident that my family piled into Robbie's car and drove to the coroner's in Southbank to identify Warren's body. We stood in a room with a large window covered by a curtain on the other side. Then, when we were ready, the curtain opened, and there lay my darling brother, lifeless on a metal trolley, covered in a white sheet, except for his face.

I will never forget the guttural sound of grief that filled the room.

The following days were spent at Robbie's house, organising the funeral. On the Sunday, my boss called and said it would be best for me to go to work on Monday and Tuesday before the funeral on Wednesday, to keep my mind busy. I don't know why, but I went in. I was a receptionist and had to answer up to 200 calls a day. The receptionist from our Sydney office called and asked why I was there. I told her what my boss suggested. She was astounded. I am, too, and I can't believe I was so naive as to follow those orders.

On the day of the funeral, I went in to view Warren's body in a separate room before the ceremony. His skin was waxy-looking, and there was a strange protrusion on his forehead (I later learned what that was from after reading the coroner's report, which contained detailed information of his injuries). His hands were stiff and sitting unnaturally on his lap. The mortician had dressed him in a white shirt and black pants that didn't suit his personality. I kissed him on his cold forehead and slipped my 21st birthday invitation into his chest pocket. My party was in a few weeks.

My cousin Mark gave me the biggest hug back outside in the sunshine. So many of my friends came to support me, and an ex-boyfriend was there. That meant a lot to me as he knew Warren, and I felt a special closeness to those that knew him. In the days after Warren died, I felt his presence behind me at all times, like he was floating near my shoulders. After the funeral, he was gone. I imagined him protecting me to ensure I got through those difficult days.

I had my 21st birthday party three weeks later. It was difficult to celebrate when our family was so broken, but it went ahead anyway. We didn't celebrate Christmas that year, and I went camping with my boyfriend and spent Christmas day floating on a lilo in a river somewhere in northeast Victoria.

Over the following years, we awaited the court case to find out if the truck driver would be convicted. The case was heard at the Moe Magistrates Court rather than in Melbourne, as it was closer to the driver's home. Yes, the court thought it would be best to make it easy for the man that killed Warren, not for Warren's family. We all took days off work and drove down twice only to be told after we arrived that the case had been adjourned. Finally, on the third date, a judge heard the case. As we waited in the waiting room just outside the courtroom we were to enter, a police officer sat opposite us, casually flicking through photos from the scene of the accident. The anger and disgust I felt towards him were immense. We found out later that a different police officer quit the force after the way the police handled the case. One has to question what happened for that officer to quit, but we never found out.

During the case, we heard from two witnesses. One was an 18-year-old male who had stopped at the red light. He told of seeing the truck coming up behind him, then swerving and going through the red light, hitting Warren's car. He ran to the mangled car and looked through the window. Warren looked up at him with fear in his eyes before dying. So no, coroner, he didn't die instantly. Unfortunately, that poor man will have to live with that vision for the rest of his life. Another driver also told of seeing the truck swerving before going through the red light.

When the judge questioned the driver, it came out that he didn't have a fixed address, he didn't have a Victorian driver's licence, and he had a list of priors as long as your arm. He said the car 'jumped out' at him in his official statement and that his light was green. Authorities tested the lights, and no, the light wasn't green, which matches the witnesses' testimonies. Further, other witnesses had seen the truck stopped at a fast-food outlet a few hundred metres before the intersection. I believe he was eating and didn't see the light turn red. The police checked inside the truck at the scene and found prescriptions for 'uppers', yet they never requested the driver's blood be tested.

With all this information, the law at the time only allowed the judge to charge him with manner dangerous (which I think is now known legally as driving in a manner dangerous to the public), and he received a $2000 fine. All my brother's life was worth was a measly $2000. I will never understand how that could be, how our laws are so lax that a young man's life is so undervalued. At the very least, the driver of the truck should have been charged with culpable driving causing death.

At least once a week since Warren's death, I have seen trucks from the company involved in the accident. Although he is never far from my mind, seeing these trucks reminds me of the horror Warren and our family went through. However, I do get comfort thinking about the last moment we shared. Warren had come to my house to borrow money. When he arrived, I could see he was upset. I initially thought it was because he had to seek help from his little sister, but it was far worse. His best friend had committed suicide and naturally, he was devastated. Before he left, I gave him a big hug, not knowing that it would be a memory I look back on fondly or that the emotional moment we shared would be our last. I am grateful to have been able to comfort him during such a sad time.

Warren was 23 years old. He had a lifetime ahead of him and would have been a great uncle to the many more nieces and nephews born after his death. I am sad for the life he has missed out on, and I still grieve for the brother I have lost, but I see elements of him in my children, which makes me smile.

> Grief, I've learned, is really just love.
> It's all the love you want to give, but cannot.
> All that unspent love gathers up in the corners of your eyes, the lump in your throat, and in that hollow part of your chest.
> Grief is just love with no place to go.
>
> **- Jamie Anderson**

REFLECTIONS

Nothing can prepare you for the sudden loss of a sibling, or anyone for that matter. I still think about Warren every day, nearly 24 years after his death. It took me a long time to get over the anger I felt towards the other driver, but today, I feel nothing if I think of him. I know he will be living in his own hell.

Grief doesn't leave you; it merely changes with time. I can now think of Warren without crying or getting upset, but I still get a tightness in my chest. Some days I listen to music that reminds me of him, some days I cry, but I don't feel anger anymore. Of course, I will always have a sadness within me, and I will never forget Warren, but I now choose to remember the happy times instead.

I have always said that I wouldn't wish this type of pain on anyone, yet, I do wish for understanding. Grief can be ugly and raw, but I found that friends who said something – anything – made me feel better. As Bréne Brown says in *Daring to Lead*, "Show up for people in pain, and don't look away." That small amount of discomfort you may feel in contacting someone who is grieving is momentary, but the impact you have on them will remain with them. If you don't know what to say, simply say just that. It's far better than not saying anything at all.

Dad with Warren in 1974/5.

One of my favourite photos of Warren as a toddler.

Warren and me in 1977.

Warren always loved anything with wheels – at our home in Endeavour Hills, around 1980.

Another favourite photo – Warren and me at our home in Endeavour Hills.

At 'our tree' in Dandenong, around 1985.

Warren didn't often smile for photos. I love his smirk in this one, taken around 1996.

One of the last photos taken of Warren, talking with Dad at Grandma's funeral in 1997.

The driver of this 1974 Toyota Corolla died following a collision on the corner of Army Rd and the Princes Highway, Pakenham, on Thursday night.

Second fatality at blackspot

A 23-year-old Dandenong North man died last Thursday night in a collision between a vehicle and a semi-trailer at the corner of Army Road and the Princes Highway, Pakenham.

The driver of the 1974 Toyota Corolla was turning right from Army Road onto the highway. The Scania truck was travelling east along the highway.

The accident occurred at 8.45 pm. Traffic was diverted via Ryan Road and later Seven Mile Road.

VicRoads classifies the intersection as a blackspot. At least eight accidents were reported there in the past five years. Last Thursday's fatality was the second in three years.

It is one of seven blackspots between Nar Nar Goon and the Berwick Freeway in Beaconsfield.

The Member for Pakenham Rob Maclellan has promised to speak to Roads and Ports Minister Geoff Craige.

Traffic lights were installed three years ago when the Pakenham Hills Primary School opened.

Country Fire Authority media liaison officer Tony Lucas, who was at the accident scene for more than four hours, described the intersection as very dangerous particularly for vehicles coming from Army Road.

"Many motorists who get a green light hesitate because of a fear vehicles come over the hill too quickly," he said.

He wants VicRoads to warn motorists, especially drivers of trucks, to adjust their speed as they approach the intersection.

Mr Lucas also called on VicRoads to readjust timing of the lights and improve visibility on the intersection.

Shire of Cardinia Mayor Cr Edwin Hume said each accident demonstrated the importance of the early construction of the Pakenham Bypass.

A local newspaper article about Warren's accident.

My friend Sue and me at Warren's wake.

WESTIN. — Warren James, taken from me Nov. 27, 1997. How I'll miss your caring heart and gentle smile. I'll always look up to you Wazz. You are in my heart forever big brother. — Your little sister Sharon. ♥ ♥ ♥ ♥ ♥

Above: Me, putting on a brave face at my 21st, held three weeks after Warren died.
Left: My message in the obituaries.

Above: Warren's rock and plaque at Bunurong Memorial Park in Dandenong South – Genesis Gardens, Garden Area 45, Bed 155, Boulder 063.

Left: This was taken in Carlisle, England, as my family rushed back to our car within our ticketed time frame. We turned a random corner and there it was at the entrance to the car park. Warren James, looking out for me. xx

Chapter 7

Party Like it's 1999

It actually started in 1989. I was 12 and was seated at the kids' table at my cousin's wedding. Like all the other tables, the kids' table had wine on it. I honestly don't know how much I drank, but it wouldn't have been much to get me completely drunk. All I remember is falling asleep in the car and then waking up on my couch at home with a terrible hangover. I don't remember getting in trouble; the hangover was enough punishment.

At 14, I went to my first nightclub with Robbie and his girlfriend. I was already 5'9" by that age and could walk right in without ID. I didn't drink this night but danced the night away and pashed a guy on the dance floor while *Lola* played. I felt so grown up and fell asleep with a big smile on my face.

By the age of 15, I was going to my brother's footy club on a Saturday night. I did drink here, a lot, and almost every weekend. One night, I brought a friend along, and we drank so much, we took an hour to walk about 200m to my house. My brother came to check on us and found the door wide open, and both of us sprawled on my bed, passed out and fully clothed. Around the same time, another friend and I would spend hours together at her house playing gin rummy, eating CCs and chocolate, and drinking whatever alcohol she could find in her home. She mixed a horrid cocktail of straight spirits one night, around 300-400ml, and I drank it. Surprisingly, I didn't end up in the hospital, but I was a terribly sick girl.

A little more mature at 16, my mum would buy me a flask of vodka for the weekend. Raspberry was my mixer of choice. Sometimes I would go to a friend's house or a party to drink, and other times I was at home. My best friend and I would sit in my driveway and drink until we couldn't sit straight. My boyfriend at the time was one of Robbie's friends, so I spent quite a bit of time with him. We spent one evening at one of their friend's houses. The boys played cards together, and I kept sneaking off to the kitchen to drink from one of the four bottles of scotch they brought. I emptied the entire bottle. Again, I didn't end up in the hospital, but I can still almost feel the coldness of the toilet bowl I got to know intimately that night. I haven't been able to bear the smell of any brown spirit since.

When I was legally allowed to drink, I was at nightclubs every Thursday night and usually at least once on the weekend. The club I frequented on a Thursday was with my boyfriend and all his footy mates, schoolmates, and partners. We took up one entire side of the club and always stayed in the same area. We knew everyone there, including the bar staff, so I was utterly shocked to pass out after having only one drink. It was sudden, and it scared everyone around me. My boyfriend tried to catch me by grabbing my jeans, but the belt loop snapped with the force of my fall. I can only recall snippets, like photos flashing in front of me – my boyfriend and his best mate on either side of me, walking through a crowd; the security guard helping us down the back stairwell; the neon lights as we walked to the car...

The next day, I wrote my mum's phone number on my hand in texta, fearing I may pass out again on the way to school. I fell asleep on the bus and had a dream. In the dream, I was looking out of the bus's windscreen, sitting in the same seat on the bus I was travelling on. Everything was a bit fuzzy and awash in red. I saw a man get on the bus and awoke suddenly. I shook my head to clear away the fog of tiredness, and moments later, that same man got on the bus. I had seen something yet to happen in real life and I was scared. I started to wonder if someone had spiked my drink the night before. A month later, I passed out at the same club after just one drink again. This time, my boyfriend caught me.

I went to the doctors the next day, and they said if I were drugged, it would no longer be in my system, so there was no point in testing my blood. Even after these incidents, I still went back to the same club, but thankfully it never happened again.

My 21st party was held at Moorabbin Airport three weeks after Warren died. I don't know how we managed it as a family, but we all made it happen. Not all went to plan. The DJ was two hours late, so Robbie made him play the extra time when the party was supposed to have ended. Robbie did a speech, followed by my closest male friends, which was lovely and a little cheeky. I found it hard to enjoy the night. How could I? I smiled, did my speech, and thanked everyone, but there was a darkness hanging over my family and me. Similarly, my 40th birthday was a few months after Dave died. Again, I had the party, because I wanted to look forward to something. It was great to see so many friends and family, and I couldn't have managed without their help. I possibly didn't need the vodka shot just before I did my speech, though. Thanks, Baz!

A couple more years of nightclubbing, combined with smoking joints, are all a bit of a blur. It got worse after Warren died. I drank as much as I could every time I went out. I had to numb the pain and grief. I tried to fill the emptiness inside me with alcohol, drugs, and sex. Anything to not feel the deep pain in my soul. I could drink almost any of my male friends under the table and go back and do it all again the next night and the next.

I didn't partake in drugs too much, alcohol was my drug of choice, but I did try cocaine twice. The first time was on a nightclub's roof with a friend's friend. We used a $20 note. The second time was after a very eventful night. A girlfriend picked me up from the airport after a trip to Queensland. We stopped at a bar to have a cocktail on the way home. We then went home, got dolled up, and headed into the city to a club where another friend was the bar manager. You know what that means – free drinks! Before this venue turned into a proper nightclub, it was a male review show. I almost fell off my barstool when I recognised one of the dancers, a guy from my brother's footy club, who I pashed one drunken night a few years earlier. Hilarious! There were so many women near the stage, screaming for the hot bodies, that we would usually sit at the back of the bar, but this time, we sat near the front.

To my horror, I got called up on stage. It was awful. If someone is going to put their penis near my face, they should at least buy me a drink first!

After the show finished and the venue transformed into a club, my friends and I were having a great time dancing and drinking when some cuties joined us. They were a group of around 12 guys out on a bucks night. After way too many drinks, we were invited to continue the party back at Crown Casino. They had three hotel rooms, on three floors, all immediately on top of each other. We drank some more, went from room to room via the stairs in the hallway, and eventually, one of the guys offered me some cocaine. I accepted. I had never seen so much cocaine. I didn't have much, but it was more than enough for me. I was flying high for the next 12 hours. After the sun rose, my friend and I got a taxi home, and I went and did my grocery shopping. I was sure everyone in the store knew what I had been up to.

Eventually, my drinking had to come to an end. It was getting out of control. The pivotal moment happened on Melbourne Cup day, almost a year after Warren died. The drinking started before 9 am and continued throughout the day. After the Cup, we moved on to a bar; I don't recall where and I didn't make it inside. I realised I needed to get home and called a friend to pick me up. He was disappointed in me; I could see it on his face. He drove me home, back to a house I was sharing with two old school friends. They were having a party. I couldn't bear to join in even though some of my closest friends were there. I went to my room and played a song that reminded me of Warren, full blast and on repeat. I sang and cried until I passed out on my bed.

After so much dangerous behaviour, I decided to tone down the drinking and am so grateful that I did. I met Andrew, had kids, and didn't drink much for many years. In the last year of my marriage, I started drinking more again. There were a few nights of drinking too much, and then I had another drunken breakdown. Four of us went to the Cold Chisel concert at Rochford Wines. I was so looking forward to it as I hadn't seen them live before. It was raining, and we couldn't lay out our preprepared cheese platter. What else could we do but drink? And so I did – three plastic carafes of Prosecco, and I sadly have no memory of the mighty voice of Jimmy Barnes. A whole chunk of time disappeared. The next thing I remember is hanging out the window being violently ill. Class all the way. I was incredibly embarrassed and ashamed, and the following day I messaged the people we went with to apologise.

I still enjoy a drink now and then, but (mostly) in moderation. I have drunk enough to last a lifetime.

> Here's to the nights we don't remember
> and the friends we won't forget.
>
> – 'The Hangover'

REFLECTIONS

I'm not proud of taking drugs, and thankfully it never became a problem for me. If I wasn't always skint, things might have been different. Unfortunately, my family has the addiction gene, so I have needed to make good choices. It only takes one bad choice for you to cross the invisible line to addiction.

I didn't make many good choices when it came to alcohol. Not only is alcohol detrimental to your physical body, the toll it takes on your mental health is undeniable. At the time, a low blood alcohol concentration can make you feel happy, more confident and reduce your inhibitions, but it also affects your judgement. The higher it goes, the more likely you are to have impaired balance, vision, and coordination, as well as your emotions becoming less stable. In addition, there's a high chance of injury to yourself or someone else, unprotected sex, or worse, unwanted sex. The long-term effects on your body can include mental health issues, brain damage, cirrhosis of the liver, increased risk of various cancers, and weight gain, which comes with a plethora of its own complications.

If you need a way to make you feel better, I suggest trying some of the following services (Australia only):

Alcoholics Anonymous   www.aa.org.au   1300 222 222

Alcohol and Drug Foundation   www.adf.org.au   1300 85 85 84

Family Drug Support   www.fds.org.au   1300 368 186

For support in other areas of your life, see the list in Chapter 11.

Me aged 2 or 3.

Me at our family Christmas, moments before I rested my head on the microphone for a drunken little nap, aged 15.

Ben, Brooke, Scott, and Basil (front), and me (back) at Brooke's 40th, Melbourne Cup 2016. I drank almost an entire bottle of vodka and didn't see a horse all day. We even managed to get our pic on the nightly news.

Above: Year 12 muck up day. I started drinking around 8 am.

Right: Before I was too drunk to use my phone, at Cold Chisel's concert – A Day on the Green, Rochford Wines, 2020.

Chapter 8

Our Rocketman

Dave was my eldest brother but also like a father figure to me. He was the man of the house, and from a young age, showed a strong work ethic. His first job was a paper round at the age of 11. He started as a butcher's apprentice and became qualified by 18. Before school, Warren and I would get up in the wee hours and go with Mum to take him to work at Fountain Gate. He then started a boilermaker apprenticeship at Mum's workplace. During that apprenticeship, he had a terrible accident. The foreman told him to use an empty drum as a seat. Soon after he started using it, the drum exploded. It wasn't empty. It had a small amount of thinners in it. He was very fortunate, mainly only receiving burns to his face. Thankfully, these burns healed well and weren't noticeable later in life. He remained in that industry until an injury stopped him in his mid-40s. As a butcher, he had regular knife injuries resulting in multiple visits to the doctor or ER for stitches. His hands showed how hard he worked. They were strong and worn hands.

Growing up, he always looked out for me. He would come home from work, throw the change from his pocket on the floor of his bedroom, and go cook a steak. He would often let Warren and I go and gather up the coins to put in our money boxes. He was always offering money in later years if I needed it, even if he didn't have much leftover for himself, and rarely accepted a payback. Once I owed him $500. When I gave it back to him in $100 notes, he turned to my two kids and his three kids at the time and handed them each one. He would lend me his car when I needed it, and one day drove from Dandenong to Elsternwick to jump-start the vehicle I borrowed. I had accidentally left the lights on.

Dave was a bloke but also had a gentle side. He was a funny man, pulling pranks and always making you laugh. We would often talk to him and find he had some 'Billy Bob' teeth in, making it hard to take him seriously. However, he would put his hand up to help anyone, even strangers, once stopping traffic on a busy main road to help a postie pick up the mail he had dropped.

After Warren died, Dave regularly contacted the owner of the company whose truck was driven in the accident, to request they help pay for a memorial plaque at Bunurong Memorial Park. Initially, they said no, but Dave wouldn't take no for an answer. He continued calling the owner until he gave in. Thanks to Dave, Warren has his plaque in a beautifully peaceful setting, on a rock next to a lake. We could never have afforded it, and I am forever grateful to Dave and his tenacity to get that done.

Dave also spoke to lawyers for years, fighting to get some form of compensation for our family after Warren's accident. Finally, eight years after Warren died, through mountains of paperwork and a court hearing, we were each awarded $20,000 through Victims of Crime, as well as a handful of therapy sessions. I was pregnant with Connor at the time, and that money was beneficial for our young family. Like me, Dave struggled with injustice, and he would continue a fight until justice was served. He fought for his family; he fought for strangers; he fought for his community.

On the 5th of August, 2016, around 4 pm, I received a text message from Leonie, Dave's partner, to say that he was in the hospital and has cancer. I called back immediately, and she apologised for the message but was unable to call. There were no accurate details at this stage as the doctors weren't yet sure what type of cancer he had, and had initially diagnosed him with diabetes. Dave said I could come in the next day to see him. I started thinking back over the last few months. He had started a job at Bunnings, had four kids – one was a sprightly two-year-old boy – and was 47 years old, so him being tired didn't ring any alarm bells. Since I had seen him, though, he had lost a dramatic amount of weight.

The following day, I went to see Dave in Dandenong hospital. Leonie was also there. Dave drifted in and out due to the pain medication he was on. Not knowing what was ahead of us, I held Leonie, kissed her on the forehead, and told her we would get through this together. After leaving the hospital, I burst into tears. I was utterly heartbroken seeing my once strong big brother so vulnerable and unwell. After that, I went and saw him almost every day, occasionally bringing in homemade meals, soft enough to not hurt his throat, and sometimes I took my boys in to visit. They made get-well cards, and I took in the itinerary of my upcoming overseas holiday so he could see where we were going. He kept telling me to go on holiday and that he would be here when we got back. I was already making plans in my head about how our family would navigate our trip if the worst were to happen.

Eventually, he was diagnosed with oesophageal cancer. On the 14th, the doctors moved him to the cancer ward at another hospital. This hospital was closer to me but further for Leonie and the kids, making it harder on her. I asked Dave if there was anything I could bring him, and he asked for the apple slice that my mother-in-law made. She promptly delivered the dessert, and he enjoyed it the next day. He was so grateful for that.

Every time I visited, he would proudly introduce me to the other people in his shared room and the nurses. We would spend time holding hands, him lying on his bed and me in a chair pushed up close to him. Sometimes we talked, sometimes we sat in silence, and sometimes I watched him as he dozed off. I would rub his back and eventually brought in a massage ball to help ease his pain.

After much organisation, on the 21st, I picked Dave up from the hospital, along with any medication and strict instructions from the nurses, and drove him out to Casey Fields to watch his son play in his footy grand final. He wanted to walk, even though I had a wheelchair for him. He tried to be upbeat but was so unwell. He managed to stay until the end of the game, and I promptly took him back to the hospital after. The whole trip there and back, the thought of something going wrong kept going over and over in my head. I had planned out what I would do if that were to happen.

On the 26th, he started radiation which reduced some of the tumours. But, sadly, the cancer had spread to his stomach and liver, and the tumour in his liver was aggressive. The doctors said that if the radiation worked, he may have had up to eight weeks left and if it didn't, it would be as little as two weeks. It was now terminal. I was at the GP trying to sort out Mitchell's cough before our trip when I received that call. I tried to contain myself, and after the GP had tended to Mitchell, she asked the kids to leave and checked if I was OK. I told her what was happening, and she gave me a big hug and said to come back anytime. Andrew had flown to Queensland that morning to help his parents bring back their caravan, so it was just the boys and me. We camped out in the lounge the whole weekend and ate junk food and watched movies, and all the while, I was keeping my family up-to-date through messages. The support I received from cousins and aunts during this time was so needed and much appreciated.

Both Dave and I hadn't been in contact with Mum or Robbie for years. I asked if he wanted to tell them that he was sick, and he said no. If Dave had said yes, I would have personally told either of them. It wasn't until the 27th that he changed his mind and said it was OK to tell Robbie, so Joanne told him.

Saturday 27th saw many family members visit, and I know Dave was so grateful for that. It was hard for him to show it due to his fatigue and pain, but he was so happy to see everyone. We all spent hours in the guest's area talking and reliving old times.

On Sunday 28th, he was allowed to go home for the day. Leonie picked him up, and they spent time together as a family, before taking him back to the hospital later in the day.

At around 7.30 am on Monday 29th, Leonie called to say the doctor had called her into the hospital because Dave wasn't doing well. As I was closer, I said I would go straight in and for her to get there when she could. When I arrived at the hospital, I was not prepared for what I would walk in on. Dave was slumped at the end of his bed, vomiting out the blackness of cancer into a plastic vomit bag held by a nurse. There were two doctors in the room, a younger female doctor and a senior male doctor. They wouldn't give me any information as I wasn't his next of kin, just his sister. They wanted to wait for Leonie to arrive, which she did around an hour later. While I waited for Leonie, I was continually helping Dave up and down from his bed, trying to help him get comfortable. No staff assistance was given. At one stage, when I was holding him up, I looked him in the eye and said, "You know I will look after Leonie and the kids," and he replied, "Why? What have the doctors said?" I said, "Nothing darling, I just want you to know."

After Leonie arrived, and Dave was as comfortable as he could be, we sat down next to his bed and spoke with the doctors about a potential drug trial. I don't know if Dave could hear us when we were talking. The senior doctor had a terrible bedside manner, and at one point, I held my hand up towards his face and told him to put his manners back in. I told him to treat Leonie with the respect she deserved. After much back and forth with the senior doctor, he finally called to organise the drug. On the phone to another doctor, he said with disdain that he was doing his public rounds and went on to talk about a recent round of golf. This was all before even mentioning the reason for the call. It would cost $5000, and we would have to transport Dave ourselves to another hospital to administer it. They wouldn't send him in an ambulance as they feared that he would die, simply by moving him.

After the doctors left the room, I followed them out. I asked how long they thought he would have if he didn't get the drug. I said, "Are we talking weeks or days here?" The senior doctor scoffed, looked at me like I was an idiot, and said, "Hours." I then asked if I should get his kids to the hospital, and he said yes. Not once during the many hours we had spent together that morning had anyone told us how gravely ill Dave was. We had no idea that this was it. Obviously, we knew he didn't have much time left, but no one had clearly said the words. I walked back into the room, hugged Leonie, and said, "Sweetie, this is it, it's happening. We need to get the kids here."

The nurses moved Dave to a larger single room at the end of the corridor, which I now understand to be the farewell room. It was large enough to accommodate a big group of people. The palliative care nurses medicated Dave to make him comfortable, and he never truly regained consciousness.

While Leonie called her family, I rang her sister-in-law to ask her to pick up Daniel, as she had a car seat. I also rang the kid's school to let them know what was happening and that Katelyn would come by to pick up Sarah. Brendon was already home. The lady on the phone was lovely and understanding, but when Katelyn arrived, she made her call Leonie to verify that it was, in fact, true and that she wasn't just taking Sarah out to go shopping. Really...

By the time all the kids arrived, it was around 1 pm. I had been at the hospital since 8 am. Those hours were forever lost through the lack of communication by the doctors. Family started arriving, and we all stood around, taking turns to hold Dave's hand. Robbie came to the hospital, and I saw him for the first time in seven years. He gave me a big hug and went in to see Dave. Robbie was so gentle and loving, kissing Dave on the forehead and holding his hand. The nurses, who were compassionate and gentle with us, suggested we play his favourite music and explained that he could still hear us. Katelyn played one of his favourites, Elton John. Leonie spent the day curled up on the bed beside the love of her life, her arm around him, holding hands. I tried to stay busy checking on the kids and making sure everyone was OK. I felt I had been able to say my farewell to Dave that morning and wanted everyone else to have their moment with him.

By this stage, Dave had 17 of his closest family members in the room surrounding him with love. I am uncertain if I allowed my kids in before he passed away. I think I did, but I sent them home. The day was so emotional that neither Andrew nor I could remember. Twice, while lying there, heavily sedated and having not been able to communicate since the early morning, Dave clearly said, "I love you all." We were all shocked but happy to hear his voice one last time. I can still hear it. At one point, while the nurses were in the room, he sat bolt upright, stared at me with a look of fear in his eyes, before being further medicated.

At approximately 3.25 pm, he started making a terrible gurgling sound. In a panic, I called for the nurses. They rushed in and told us this was it. The sounds of grief filled the room. We were all crying and saying I love you. He slipped away at around 3.30 pm. After he died, the nurses cleaned him up. They dressed him in fresh clothes, a black t-shirt given to him the day before by our cousin Justin.

When I went in to see him, he looked so peaceful, without a wrinkle on his face. He was no longer in pain.

Within half an hour, I was on the phone to the funeral home. I needed to be sure we could organise the funeral before Saturday when I would leave to go to Europe for five weeks. The lady at the funeral home was so compassionate and did everything in her power to help make that happen. I messaged Andrew and said he could bring the kids in now. I wanted to allow them to say goodbye and see their cousins and aunty. Robbie eventually left the hospital to go and tell Mum that Dave had died. At around 7.00 pm, Joanne told us that Mum was coming to the hospital to see Dave. I had to leave. There was no way I could manage seeing her after all the day's emotions. I kissed the kids and Leonie and left the hospital.

That night, I had to catch up on my work and let my clients know I had to have the rest of the week off. I was fortunate that everyone was so understanding, but I still had to spend time collating files to send off to my clients or other designers to complete. I had friends drop off food and check on the kids. We spent the following three days organising the funeral, writing the eulogy, making sure everyone had appropriate clothes, and packing the kids' luggage in preparation for our trip. I collated photos, created the video memorial, typed up all the speeches, and designed the order of service.

I had so many messages and calls of support. My friends, family, and in-laws supported me through that horrendous week. I had only slept around three hours a night for the previous three weeks and was running on fumes. My body was so stressed and tired on the morning of the funeral, I rang the osteo in tears and managed to get an appointment to help ease my physical pain.

Later, we arrived at Leonie's, and everyone looked so lovely. Dave would have been so proud of Leonie and the kids. They were coping as well as expected but far better than I could have. Joanne had organised a limousine, and most of us piled in to get to the Stratus Chapel at Bunurong Memorial Park. I was concerned that Mum would make a scene and had family on backup to intervene if necessary.

When we arrived, I was overwhelmed with emotion, seeing some dear friends and their parents supporting me. Another old friend came out, and I fell into his arms. Then, finally, it was time to go in and Pink Floyd's *Wish You Were Here* started playing. The chapel was nearly overflowing with approximately 400 people – kids in their footy jackets, the netball team Dave coached, old friends. Around 50 of his workmates from Bunnings lined the walls, all in uniform. It was incredible. Dave would have been embarrassed that there was such a fuss for him.

The funeral was perfect, except for the celebrant not mentioning Mum. We hadn't told her not to talk about Mum and didn't have time to check her reading; we simply told her of the estrangement. There were many great stories and even a little laughter. One of the songs chosen to play during the photo reel was Elton John's *Rocketman*. It has since become Dave's song, and it's been incredible how many times I have turned the radio on just as it's beginning.

Mum was whisked away by Robbie immediately after the ceremony, but he did find me first and gave me a big hug. I said to him, "I can't believe we've had to do this again." During the wake, I sat with two friends from high school, Brooke and Kate. I was spent and my head ached. Some people came over to give their condolences and I will forever be grateful to them for that. Others stayed away, not talking to me at all. When the wake was over, we once again piled into the limousine. This time, the driver put the music and lights on, with our permission, and the kids were relaxed enough to laugh. It was so lovely to see. Leonie and I sat next to each other and held hands the whole way back to her house.

Andrew and I decided it was time to leave and got home at around 8 pm. I still had to pack my suitcase, and my dear friend Jodie had offered to come over and assist. As a seasoned traveller, she was a great help in deciding what I needed to take and gave me a little pack of necessities that I would never have thought of taking. I finally climbed into bed at midnight. Andrew, myself, and the kids left at 8 am the following day to head to the airport to fly to London. I cried almost the entire flight and only slept for around an hour or two. By the time we arrived, I was like a zombie. I didn't sleep much for the rest of the trip, getting up early to work before our days began.

Dave followed us that trip, giving me signs almost everywhere we went.

Our first adventure was to Stonehenge, and in the gallery, plastered across a wall, were the words 'Wish You Were Here,' the first song played at his funeral.

When we returned home, the signs from Dave were consistent for around two years. They included our tv turning itself on at 6 am every day. A clairvoyant told me that was him and he was 'pissing himself laughing at that.' We had an owl stop by our house for the first few weeks, every time we moved. It sat on the power lines facing us like it was protecting us. We once had two owls on our antenna when we arrived home one night. I saw them as Dave and Warren, watching over my family. I know Dave is still watching over me, and I often face the sun with my eyes closed and think of both him and Warren.

> Sisters and brothers are the truest, purest forms of love, family and friendship, knowing when to hold you and when to challenge you, but always being a part of you.
>
> – Carol Ann Albright Eastman

REFLECTIONS

Dave was my protector, and I will forever be honoured to call him my big brother. I miss him every day. I can still hear his voice when I think of him and often still think to call him.

His strength, determination, and wonderful character live on in his four beautiful children. I see elements of him in them every time we see each other. Not only are both Leonie and myself very proud of them, I know Dave would be incredibly proud of how they have managed through such heartbreak and trauma. They have his strength, kindness, and humour, and I adore them.

If there is one thing I learnt during Dave's brief stay in the hospital, it is essential to ask questions, no matter how silly they may seem to you. If I hadn't asked that question of the doctors on the day Dave died, his kids might have missed seeing him one last time.

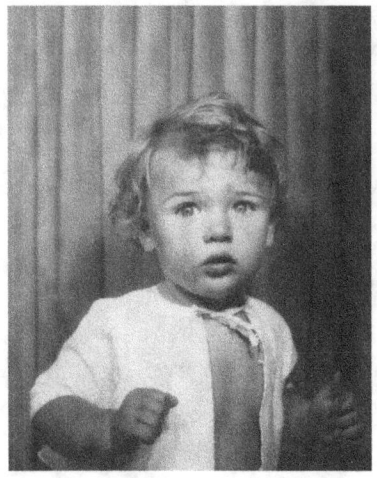
Dave was such a gorgeous little man, here as a toddler.

Always the proud big brother, 1977.

Warren, Dave and me, 1978.

Dave and me at our cousin Mark's wedding to Cindy.

Me, Grandma and Dave, 1990.

Dave and me, drunk at our family Christmas dinner, 1991.

Above left: Dave walking me down the aisle at my wedding, 2004.

Above: Dave and me on Mother's Day, 2009.

Left: Dave with Connor, 2007.

Below left: Mitch and Dave at Healesville Sanctuary, around 2012.

Below: Dave with Mitch at his first birthday party.

Dave was an adoring uncle to all his nieces and nephews.

Soulmates – Dave with the love of his life, Leonie.

Dave with his eldest child, Katelyn.

Dave with his 'Pookie', Sarah, around 2004.

Dave was so proud of all his kid's achievements – at home with Brendon, 28 August, 2016, the day before Dave passed away.

Dave with his kids, 2013.

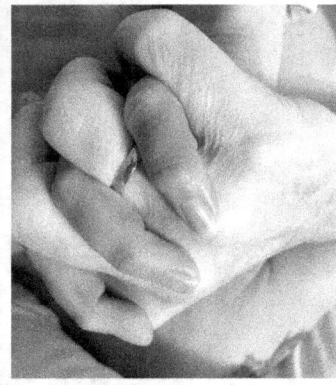

Dave with his youngest boy, Daniel, 2013.

Everlasting love. Leonie holding Dave's hand on the day he died, 2016.

Me, Connor, Mitch and Andrew, heading to Europe, the day after Dave's funeral, 3 September, 2016.

Some of the signs I saw on our trip in 2016, reminding me Dave was with us.

Relay for Life, 2016.

Leonie and the kids, and Andrew, me and the boys at Bali Zoo, after having breakfast with the orangutans on what would have been Dave's 50th birthday, 8 January, 2019.

A sign in a restaurant in Bali. Dave was with us here too!

There was a small rock beside Warren's memorial and the staff dug to check if it could work as a memorial for Dave. They were shocked to see how big the rock actually was. They dug it out and created this area for our family. My two angel brothers, together. Dave's rock can be found in the Genesis Gardens, Garden Area 45, Bed 155, Boulder 065

This is how I will always remember Dave. x

Chapter 9

Sister-Not-Sister

In 2016, after Dave passed away, I began thinking more about Cheryl. I started to wonder whether I should try to track her down somehow. Time went by, and in 2018, I reached out to my cousin Kathleen on my father's side. I don't know the Westin side of the family, and I hadn't seen Kathleen, or anyone on that side, since my grandmother's funeral in March of 1997. It must have been at least 11 years since I'd seen anyone before that. So, I asked if anyone on that side of the family knew anything about Cheryl. They did know of her, of course, but they had no further details to help me. I didn't know how else to find her, and although I let it go for the moment, I thought of Cheryl often.

On a Sunday afternoon in August 2020, as Andrew was packing to leave the family home, I found the article that my mum showed me so many years prior. I was happy to find a missing piece of the puzzle. I read through the article again, as distressing as it was, to find any other names that may help me in my search. The only details I had were Cheryl's name and her mum's. I could work out her birth year from further information in the article. The following day, I started searching online.

I continued searching through to Thursday. On Thursday evening, I received a message from my cousin Kathleen, whom I contacted a couple of years before. It said, "Hi Sharon, I hope you're well. I have just been contacted by someone on ancestry saying she is Ronnie's daughter." The timing was incredible. I felt like it was meant to be. She went on, "She would like to get in touch." I told my cousin that Cheryl could connect with me through Facebook if she wanted to. I'm not sure why I didn't give her my number straight away. We were messaging within minutes, sharing photos and stories. There was so much to take in, and after realising it would take more than a message, I gave her my number. We talked on the phone only half an hour after that first message from my cousin. My mind was spinning, and my heart was whole.

It was a little unusual at first, but I immediately felt connected. It felt so good to give Cheryl some details that were missing from her life. I even had photos of her as a baby in my possession. Cheryl hadn't known that I existed before doing her DNA test and connecting with the Westin side of the family. I had to explain that it wasn't just me, she had a brother as well, in Warren, and that he had died in 1997. We talked for two solid hours and agreed that as soon as the state's restrictions were eased (due to the COVID-19 pandemic), I would drive to her house in Geelong to meet her. We stayed in touch over the following month, and finally, in November, I went to meet my long-lost half-sister.

There were no nerves, as it honestly felt like we already knew each other. I ended up staying two nights, and it was perfect. We learned a lot about each other's lives, shared photos, and met up for a drink with our cousin. Kathleen gave us even more details about the Westin side of our family that I had never known. The most surprising information was that Westin is a Swedish name. I had never known this and had never thought to research it. I thought our family was Australian, going back multiple generations, with British roots. That is why I did the DNA test in the first place. Cheryl and I continued to stay in contact, and I visited the following month again.

On 21 January 2021, my DNA test results came in. You know the rest of that story from the introduction. Cheryl and I remain in contact, and we affectionately call each other sister-not-sister.

Cheryl and I the night we met, 2020.

Cheryl and I at the pub, waiting to see our cousin Kathleen, 2020.

REFLECTIONS

I am so incredibly grateful to now have Cheryl in my life. Although it's now apparent we aren't related by blood, Cheryl and I are bonded forever by our shared brother Warren. I am sad that Cheryl never got to meet him, or her father Ronnie, but I know I have been able to provide some answers and clarity for her and that makes me happy.

We are also bonded by our individual stories that have crossed paths. Cheryl has supported me through my recent upsets and I am so happy to have finally met the woman I have thought about since I was a child.

Family isn't always blood. It's the people in your life who want you in theirs; the ones who accept you for who you are. The ones who would do anything to see you smile and who love you no matter what.

- Unknown

Chapter 10

An Apple A Day

MIGRAINES

I was a relatively healthy kid, only having chickenpox and measles, which was pretty standard for the time. As I got older, I began getting headaches and, at first, was given Panadol. When the headaches got worse, Mum would provide me with codeine. It soon became two codeine tablets. I then began to rely on them for even minor headaches and would go to school and work with a codeine-fogged mind. My headaches turned to migraines, the first occurring when I was 19, and I still suffer from them now. Eventually, I was getting them every two weeks, and after much research, I decided to get a Daith piercing. It's a rod that goes through a pressure point in your ear. It was excruciatingly painful to have done, and my body reacted by hitting the person doing the piercing. She was fine; it's happened before. Thankfully, the piercing did its job, and I now only get a migraine every two months or so.

TONSILLITIS AND PENICILLIN

In year 11, I started to have other health issues. I contracted tonsillitis for the first time. I was laid out on my bed, which was the couch in the lounge room, for a solid week and lost 10 kilos. Mum finally took me to the doctor, who said, "I'm glad you brought her in because her throat has almost closed." Mum thought I was faking. He jabbed my bottom with penicillin and sent me home with a script. I was well again until late in year 12. Over 12 weeks, and right in the middle of my final CATs, I got tonsillitis eight times. A day after I finished the course of antibiotics, it came back again and again.

A few months later, I had a bad cold and tonsillitis. I felt so rotten but wanted to go out with my boyfriend and his mates to see one of their dad's band play. We decided I could go as it wasn't going to be a busy venue and I could sit whilst there. On the way, I started having a coughing fit and began itching all over. I didn't know what was happening. The rest of the night is a blur, and I see it in my head as Polaroid snaps. Being rushed back to the car. Vomiting out the window at a red light. On my couch asking someone to take my shoes off because I couldn't breathe with them on (delirium setting in, perhaps). In the car park at a hospital with my mum, my boyfriend and one of his friends. On a hospital bed, vomiting into the blue kidney dish my boyfriend was holding. That's all I remember.

From all accounts, my lips had turned blue, and I was in the middle of an anaphylactic reaction to penicillin. I had been given so much over the previous 18 months that my body rejected it. Somebody told me a few days later that I was close to dying. I still wonder why no one thought to call an ambulance for me.

I finally had my tonsils out a year later, at 19. It would be the first of many operations.

WISDOM TEETH

That same year, I started to feel pain around my left ear on Christmas eve. As the night progressed, the pain moved to under my jaw. I couldn't feel any lumps, so after a couple of beers, I had some Panadol and went to sleep. Christmas morning, I woke with terrible pain and a swollen jawline. I told Mum I'd be OK and we should still go to her boyfriend's family's house for lunch. My jaw became so swollen during the day that I could barely open my mouth to drink or eat. Early on Boxing Day morning, I woke Mum in tears; the pain was so bad. She took me to the emergency department, where they gave me pethidine and said I should go to the dental hospital the following day. I had an abscess around my wisdom tooth. I felt terrible for Mum having to try to get me into the car and up the stairs at home. I was so high after the medicine, I was a dead weight.

We went off to the dental hospital, only for the dentist to tell us I would need to go to the Royal Melbourne Hospital across the road to sort out the infection first. Mum took me to the emergency department, where they rushed me straight through to a bed and attached an IV. While Mum had gone out to the car to get something, I noticed an itch, and some welts began showing up on my arms. I looked up and could only see the curtains on either side of my bed and an empty hallway. I started yelling for help, and people came from every direction. The male nurse ripped the IV from my arm. I can only imagine what I looked like for that to happen. The doctors had given me penicillin. The drug that almost killed me a couple of years before.

After all these years, it is only now that I question why on earth I was given penicillin? Surely they were told of my allergy upon admittance to the hospital... Once that drama settled, I spent three days in the hospital to finally have my wisdom tooth taken out under general anaesthetic on my 20th birthday. Happy birthday to me! The rest of my wisdom teeth were taken out under general a few months later.

GYNAECOLOGICAL HEALTH

Not long after this, I had my first pap smear. It was a horrendous experience with the elderly doctor doing a biopsy without discussing it or talking me through the procedure. I had no idea what was going on. The results came back and showed I had Cervical Intraepithelial Neoplasia (CIN) 3, the most severe before it turns to cancer. I found a new gynaecologist, a most lovely man, and he booked me in for a D&C (dilation and curette). I was 22. At 23, I went back to the gynaecologist after experiencing severe pain in my abdomen during my period and intercourse. He suspected endometriosis, and again I was booked in for surgery. I had a laparoscopy and colposcopy to have the endometriosis lasered. It worked, but he said I might find it difficult to get pregnant.

MORTON'S NEUROMA

At the age of 27, doctors booked me in for another surgery. I had severe pain and swelling in my left foot for the past seven years.

It started in my left hip and gradually moved down to my knee. I saw a physio and received ultrasound treatment to no avail. The pain then moved to my foot. It got so bad that I had to use a walking stick. After seeing a specialist, I was sent for an MRI and then told I had a Morton's Neuroma, which is a lump on a nerve in my foot. They gave me a cortisone injection in the top of my foot. Boy, did that hurt! It did last two years before I needed another, but that one only lasted a year. The next lasted six months and the next another six months. The only available treatment now was surgery.

So off I went, under the guidance of doctors, to have the surgery. They didn't find anything except scar tissue from the injections. They cleared that away but said the pain would likely come back and that two of my toes would be numb for the rest of my life. Trying to get me up and about before I was ready, the doctors forced me to stand and try to weight bear. I told them I wasn't prepared, but they wouldn't listen. Finally, I stood up, feeling like I would pass out. I looked down to see blood seeping through the bandages around my wound. They rushed to help me back onto the bed, no apology for not listening. The reopened part is now a much more unsightly scar than the rest. My two toes are still numb, and if I am on my feet for too long, my foot aches and my two numb toes burn. I haven't been able to wear heels ever since and had to give away my beautiful collection of shoes.

PREGNANCY

I continued seeing my gynaecologist. When I was engaged, he suggested that we try straight away if I wanted to have children due to my history of endometriosis. Thankfully, first try, first baby, and second try, second baby. All went well during my first pregnancy. I felt great, and the baby was growing well. Then, early one Sunday morning, I went to the toilet, and my water broke. This was it! We called the hospital, and the midwife told us there's no rush, but we should start to get ready and make our way to the hospital. On the hospital bed, my water really broke, and I watched as my pink pants changed from light to dark.

The midwives were fantastic and offered me gas as my labour started. The pain wasn't terrible but was getting worse. They then gave me pethidine. I wasn't dilating, so they suggested they induce me. Bang! There we go. That's how labour pain feels. I only had two full contractions before they gave me an epidural. Relief! Except I still wasn't dilating. I went through 13 hours of labour and only got to 3cm dilation. They checked the baby's vitals and discovered something was wrong, so they gave me another epidural and rushed me in for an emergency caesarean. My beautiful 9 pounds, 12 ounces firstborn had the cord around his neck and had stopped moving. Thankfully, he was born without any further complications. I, however, was a different story. As Andrew took our newborn to meet his grandparents upstairs, I remained in the theatre for the doctor to stitch my belly back together while vomiting continually for 15 minutes due to all the medication I had received during the labour and birth.

Our second born was an elective caesarean, elected by the doctors, not me. After my first delivery, they decided our second baby would be larger, and it was safer for us both to have the caesarean. So, at 38 weeks gestation, I went in to have our second child. Knowing what the epidural now felt like, and the fact the anaesthetist looked like he was 12 years old and took a long time to get the IV in, I had a panic attack, and had to be sedated. But, again, thankfully, our second boy was born without any complications.

DEPRESSION

After the birth of my second child, I became unwell with an infection in my uterus and fell into a deep depression. This wasn't new to me. I had suffered, undiagnosed, since I was 12. I was ashamed and didn't talk about it with anyone. I just kept on going, knowing it would lift eventually. It took a long time, and I wish I had sought help. I was not pleasant to be around, often having suicidal thoughts. I would imagine Andrew coming home only to find me in a bloody mess on the kitchen floor, after being called from work to pick the kids up because I hadn't. I still didn't seek help, even with these thoughts. After Warren died, I had seen a psychologist, but I was given the appointments for free through Victims of Crime and couldn't afford to continue.

It was only many years later, and after Dave died, I was offered help by the psychologist treating one of my kids. He could see I needed it, and it was the start of my healing. After numerous sessions, the psychologist sent me to the GP to get antidepressants. Eventually, after a year or so of monthly sessions, I went to an appointment smiling and didn't have much to say. He was happy for me to cease the sessions and go on with my life. I am still on antidepressants and possibly will be forever. I don't mind. I know they help me be me, and if that's what it takes, then so be it.

Going back to the undiagnosed depression, I am sure my behaviours and feelings from the age of 12 were depression. I would go into myself, not talk to friends or family, and not find joy in usual things. I would feel like nobody understood what I was going through. That sounds similar to typical teen angst, but this was more than that. The darkness would eventually lift, and I would be back to my usual self until the next time it reared its head. I self-harmed, cutting into my hand with the compass in my pencil case, and still have a scar from that time. Thoughts of suicide were regular, and yet I still felt I couldn't talk to anyone about it. Times were different in the early 90s, but thankfully now, there is far more support available for children and adults.

> People don't fake depression...
> They fake being OK.
> Remember that.
> Be kind.
>
> **- Unknown**

TINNITUS

After a stressful work experience at the age of 38, I started to hear ringing in my ears. I let it go for a week or two before going to the doctor. Finally, I was sent to a specialist and had to wait two months for the appointment. The specialist promptly told me it was tinnitus and that because I had it for two months, it was now chronic. I've had it for six years now, and I can manage it, but it's not easy. I often find it hard to hear in a noisy environment. For me, tinnitus is more than just a ringing in my ears. I have constant white noise; I can have it in one ear and not the other or both at once; I can have ringing in both and then a wavering high pitch noise on top of that. The high-pitched sounds can come on suddenly and strong, and I occasionally feel dizzy as a result.

MENOPAUSE

In late 2016, after not having had a period for well over 18 months, it came back with a vengeance. I had already started the night sweats and hot flashes of menopause, but my body had other ideas. I would get a flooding period for three weeks at a time, leaving me lethargic and sometimes embarrassed. After seeing the GP, she referred me to a gynaecologist, and he suggested that I could have an endometrial ablation to stop the bleeding, and while he was in there, I may as well have my tubes removed. Done, I liked the idea. So off I went for yet another surgery and haven't had any further issues. Well, not with my period anyway. I still get the hot flashes and night sweats.

HERNIA/S

Two years later, just before moving house, I felt an unusual bulge in my abdomen, near my belly button. With all the stresses involved in packing a house only nine months after moving in, it took me weeks to even realise that it could be a hernia. Off to the GP again for a referral to a surgeon. At my initial consultation, the doctor told me that it was an incisional hernia and he wanted to check the groin as well, just in case. I thought he was joking when he said I also had an inguinal hernia. No, he wasn't. Two hernias. I felt like I was overachieving in all the wrong places.

I booked in for my surgery to have both hernias repaired simultaneously. I could not help in any significant way in moving house and was so appreciative of all the help we received while I was out of action. The surgery went without a hitch, but my treatment in hospital afterwards was less than ideal. The orderly wheeled me on a bed into a darkened room and left me in the middle of the room, away from the call button. I woke and started feeling nauseous. I could see people off in the distance, and I called out for a nurse, but no one heard me. Thankfully, I had asked for my handbag before being taken back to the ward. I rang the hospital and told them the situation. A nurse came to me, but there was no apology. A day after surgery, with a 13cm vertical wound through my belly button and a 10cm wound across the top of my groin, I was told I had to have a shower. The nurse was abrupt and unsmiling. I said I would get up and walk there myself, as I wanted to see if

I was capable. She told me she would return to check on me but never came back. She left me to fend for myself.

ADENOMYOSIS

Now, as a 44-year-old, I have adenomyosis, which is a condition where the lining of the uterus breaks through and grows into the surrounding muscle wall. I have suffered random and severe pain from this. The first episode was so bad I ended up in the emergency room, having no idea what was causing the pain – more doctors, and more specialists. The only treatment for this is a hysterectomy, which I am booked in for in September 2021.

This will be my 11th surgery.

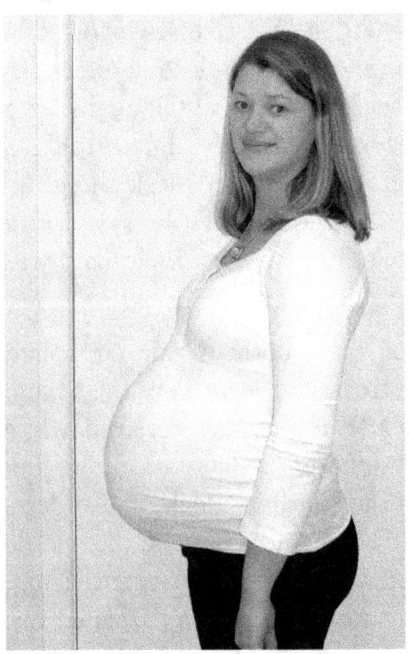

38 weeks pregnant with Connor, who was born at 41 weeks, weighing 4.5kg.

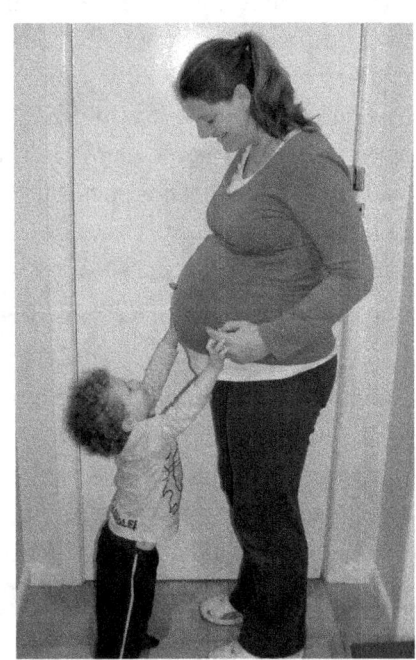

32 weeks pregnant with Mitchell, who was born at 38 weeks, weighing 4kg.

It is not the strength of the body that counts,
but the strength of the spirit.

– J.R.R. Tolkien

REFLECTIONS

Stress plays a massive role in our health. As someone who is relatively healthy, to have had, on average, one surgery every 2.2 years from the age of 19 seems an awful lot. Sure, genetics can play a part, particularly in women's health issues, but I am sure that stress has played a more prominent role. The manifestation of stress on your health is proven. Your blood pressure rises when you are stressed, and your body releases hormones, including cortisol and adrenaline. When they stay elevated through prolonged stress, your body starts to react in ways, like illness, to tell you to slow down.

Not only are there physical repercussions, the financial cost of so many surgeries also takes its toll. Running my businesses, I don't pay myself sick leave, so there are the additional lost wages on top of any out-of-pocket expenses, which can run into the thousands.

Although I have been changing the way I react to stressors in my life, they are still happening. I hope that with consistent meditation and positive thinking, my body will soon follow and give me a break from further health issues.

Another important lesson I have learnt through all this is to advocate for your health. If you feel something is wrong, speak up. I was naive to think that the doctors always had the correct answer. Knowing what I know now, I would never have had foot surgery and would have sought alternative treatments. Instead, I now see an osteopath every four weeks, have regular massages, and seek non-invasive treatments for any issues. My body, heart, and mind have been scarred, but I have come out stronger, more compassionate and now appreciate my vulnerabilities.

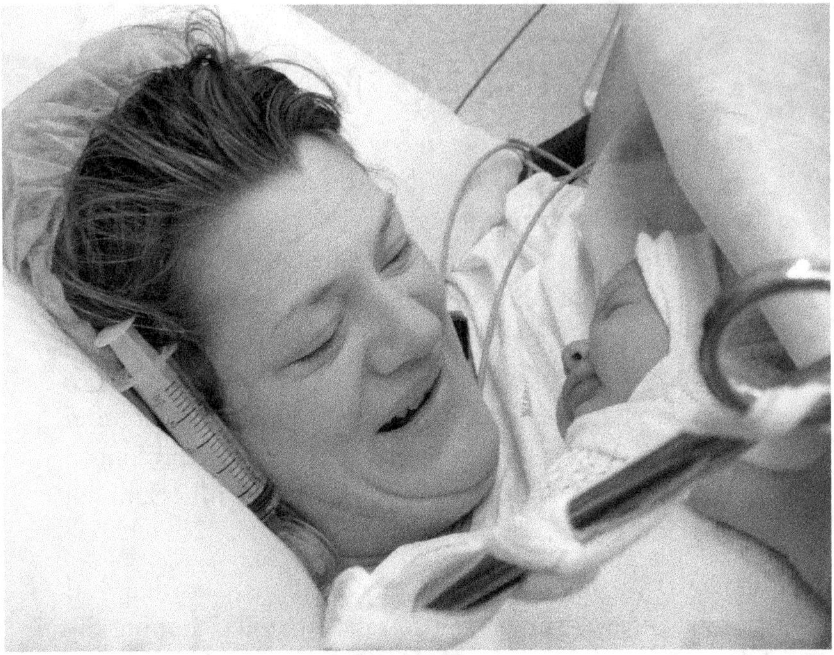

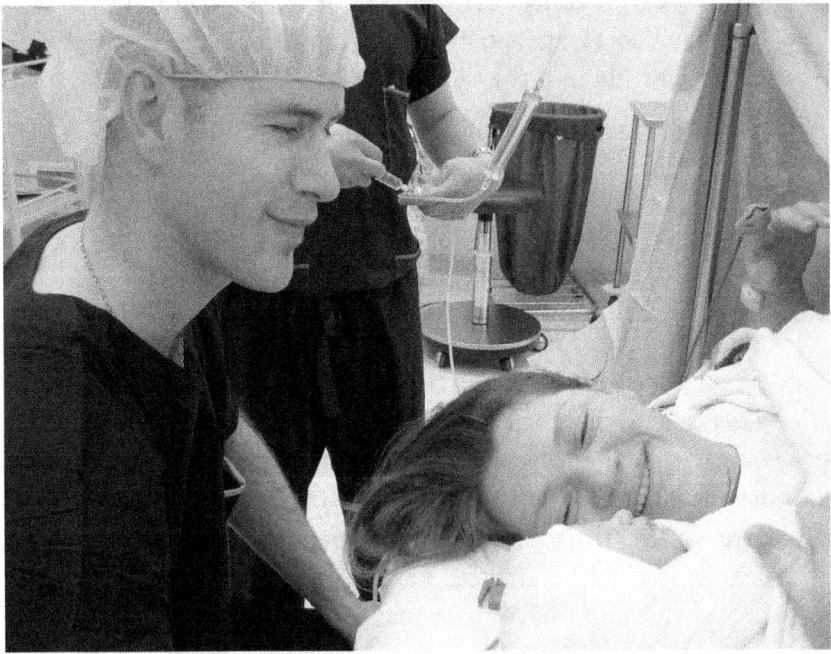

Moments after the birth of my beautiful babies. Top: Me with Connor, 2005. Bottom: Andrew, me and Mitchell, 2007.

Chapter 11

From Negative to Positive: How I Healed Myself

Life isn't meant to be one straight line, and honestly, I'd find it a little boring if it was. However, I prefer living with a positive mindset over the negative one I grew up with. It hasn't just been all the traumas that impacted me; it was also the environment and people around me. As soon as I realised what I needed, I started moving away from people that weren't part of my healing or simply weren't my people anymore.

Relationships can be complex, but when you find you are not respected and valued, or that the time has come for that relationship to run its course naturally, they no longer serve you. The people around you will either raise or lower your energy. We cannot become the person we want to be on our own, nor can we thrive around negative energy. I have chosen the people I want in my tribe, and they have been integral in my change of mindset and healing. They encourage, support, and champion me, and I hope I do the same for them.

We have but one life and I wish I had the courage and knowledge to have started to heal a long time ago. Now that I have the strength to take off the masks of my past, I am calmer, more relaxed, and finally living a life of my design.

My time is now, and I am relishing in it.

The following things have helped me heal, and I hope they can give you tips to help yourself if needed.

Please check with your medical professional to see what could work for you.

Positive Mindset

Changing negative to positive isn't as easy as it sounds. I started simply by smiling. When I am feeling down, I force myself to smile. This small act helps me reset my thoughts. Other things I have done are:

- Think of three things I am grateful for that day
- Listen to upbeat music that I can sing along to
- Read positive quotes
- Pat my dog
- Rework my thinking i.e. rather than thinking something is going to be difficult, think of how I will feel after it's done
- Surround myself with positive people, removing negative people from my life
- Celebrate the wins, even if they are small

Significant traumas aside, when a problem arises, I change my thinking from 'why is this happening to me?' to 'what is this trying to teach me?' Flipping the script and finding the silver lining instead of the black cloud has helped me search out the positive rather than automatically feeling down. I am now able to get over hurdles far more quickly than I used to.

What are you grateful for? (Don't list your family, friends, job, pet – think deeply about this.)

....

....

....

....

Find some positive quotes and write them below:

Think about a tough situation you have been in. List what you learnt from this:

Laughter

Growing up around negative people ingrained a negative mindset in me. I always wondered how some people could always appear happy, as it seemed unnatural to me. Having a good sense of humour has helped me out of many awkward situations but never long enough to change my feelings. I used my humour as a mask but have finally taken that mask off. I still am hilarious. Just ask me! I say that in jest, of course, but honestly, laughing helps relax the body and lighten your mood. When you laugh, your body releases endorphins (the feel-good chemical) into your body which eases stress and anxiety, improves your blood flow, diffuses anger, relieves tension, and much more.

I love a good comedian, satirical humour, and a good pun. Seek out what makes you laugh to help improve your happiness and your mental health. Did you know there are laughter clubs and coaches? If this is up your alley, see if there is one in your local area.

Here's a great list to show you the full benefits of laughter from my great friend Bron at Let's Laugh (www.letslaugh.com.au).

Have you ever wondered about the benefits of laughter?

Research supports the findings that it:

- Boosts the immune system
- Improves circulation
- Regulates blood pressure and increases oxygen levels in the blood
- Improves memory storage and recall, thereby increasing the ability to learn
- Mitigates anxiety
- Reduces stress
- Supports mental wellbeing
- Mitigates pain
- Increases energy levels
- Increases motivation
- Increases perceived wellbeing (happiness)

- Increases feelings of self-esteem
- Improves social connections (and mitigates loneliness)
- Is a gentle aerobic workout

and when used in business environments it:

- Boosts morale
- Increases creativity, innovation, and performance
- Improves team cohesion and creation
- Is an effective leadership skill
- Increases job satisfaction and reduces employee turnover
- Improves client connection
- Has been shown to have a positive impact on that all-important bottom line

What makes you laugh?

....
....
....
....
....
....
....

Do you have a favourite joke?

....
....
....
....
....

How can you bring laughter into your daily life?

....

....

....

....

....

Medication

I often sense I need to say, like in a therapy group, "My name is Sharon, and I have a mental illness." That's honestly what it feels like with the stigmas surrounding depression, anxiety, and other mental illnesses. So I try to break those stigmas, one conversation at a time.

My healing journey was only made possible after taking anti-depressants and talking to others about my depression. I understand medicating is not the right path for everyone, but it helped me immensely. It was like defragging a computer to clear out the excess files and reorder the ones left. I began by speaking to my GP. Thankfully, I had found a brilliant GP who treated most appointments like a mini counselling session. We would talk easily, making me feel very comfortable, and she was not judgemental. I was so happy I had finally found someone I could talk to.

I agreed that I needed medical help in changing my mood. I wish I had done it since I was 12, but it took almost 30 years to own it. I now openly tell people I am on anti-depressants, in the right situations, of course. Talking freely about suffering from depression and taking medication is the only way to break down the shame often associated with mental illness. It frees me from carrying the burden of a secret, and more often than not, talking about it helps the other person understand me better. It may even help them understand themselves better.

The road to feeling like myself again was long. It took around five to six weeks for the changes to be noticeable to me, and then I had to get used to my new normal. Finally, however, I can now see through the darkness of depression with a clear mind and bright eyes.

Have you felt sad for a few days / a week / two weeks? If the answer is yes, it's a good idea to seek professional help. Visit your GP and tell them how you're feeling.

If you can, write what caused this feeling.

....

....

....

....

....

> Your greatest growth comes from your darkest times.
> – BEN CROWE (The Imperfects Podcast, Season 3 Episode 3)

Counselling

As mentioned in the chapter 'An Apple a Day,' I was treated by a psychologist after Dave died. Talking through my problems and delving into my past hurts was incredibly difficult, but it's one of the best decisions I have made for my health and wellbeing. I understood my feelings better, which allowed me to work through them and clear the negative ones.

I found this psychologist by chance, after the one who was supposed to see my son initially didn't turn up. So if you think you need to see one, the best place to start is with a trusted GP.

Write down some questions you may have for your psychologist or GP:

....

....

....

....

....

What areas of your life would you like to talk about in your sessions?

....

....

....

....

....

Music

I have always loved music. It helps me to release emotions quickly and easily. My current anthem is *Fly Away* by Tones and I, which I play daily. Some songs still make me sad, like those played at my brothers' funerals, but I sit with those emotions and let them pass through me. I have recently discovered frequency music that uses specific tones to help stimulate the brain, balance your energy and heal you. I find them so relaxing and sometimes fall asleep listening to them.

While working, I listen to various frequency music or something gentle if I need to focus. When I need to 'get shit done,' I sometimes listen to Nirvana or some other 90s heavy rock. Spotify is the most used app on my phone, and I have playlists for all sorts of scenarios such as chill, dance, sensual, and sleep.

I also listen to podcasts regularly. Working alone, it's nice to hear a conversation. I listen to many self-help, informative, business, or funny podcasts like:

- Armchair Expert (one of my favs)
- The Imperfects
- Renegades Born
- Kwik Brain
- Unlocking Us with Brené Brown
- Dare to Lead with Brené Brown

- We Can Do Hard Things with Glennon Doyle
- No Filter (Mamamia)
- Anything with Elizabeth Gilbert!

I often ask people for recommendations, share what I have listened to, or Google 'Top podcasts in <year>,' or 'Top podcasts for <topic> in <year>.'

Who is your favourite singer or band?

What music helps you:

Relax:

Get pumped up:

Clean the house:

What are some podcasts you recommend?

What are some podcasts on your To-Listen-To list?

Art

I have been creative since I was a young child. My mum was an artist, as was my maternal grandmother who won art awards when she was young. So, you would always find me drawing, or in my teen years, also writing poetry. I studied photography and any creative classes I could during high school and only ever wanted to be a graphic designer.

Now, it's not only through my businesses, graphic design, art classes, and weekend art retreats that I find an outlet. I have returned to my passion for painting over the last two years and find it such a cathartic hobby. I can release excess energy and fill it with emotion. I even recently sold my first painting!

I believe we are all creative in some way but have mostly had it stamped out of us as we age. So, even for those who don't think they can draw or paint, I challenge you to pick up a pencil and give it a go. It could be as simple as doodling on a scrap piece of paper. You will find it relaxes your mind and opens it up to clearer thinking.

If you have lost your creative spark, here are some simple ideas to get the juices flowing again:

Do a blind contour drawing

Grab a piece of paper and a pencil, find something to draw, look at it for a minute or so, close your eyes, and start drawing something without taking the pencil off the paper. It won't be perfect, but that's part of the fun. Try drawing the same object multiple times to see the difference.

Take the artist within on a creative adventure

Try the museum or local gallery, a bookshop or antique store, a theatre show or movie. Anywhere you can observe creativity, design, and innovation. Take some time to write a list of the places you could visit.

Become bored

Remove any digital distractions and allow yourself time to daydream and think at a deeper level. Get comfy, look out the window, breathe and let your mind wander.

You can find more ideas in my set of Cards for Creativity. To find out more, visit www.artfulnessretreats.com.au/store

Meditation

This is a big one! There has been a lot of hype over the last decade about the benefits of meditation, and for a good reason. Meditation helps get you into a relaxed state, allowing you to focus and clear the clutter from your mind. It starts with concentrating on your breathing. Breath is our first medicine, after all. It's a practice you can use anytime, anywhere. It may take time to find the right breathing exercises or meditation style, but I recommend sticking with it. If you are new to meditation, search 'guided meditations' online. You may need to try a few to find one you like. There are many schools or healers that teach meditation if you prefer learning that way. If you are in Melbourne, Penny who wrote the foreword is ah-mazing!

Meditation isn't just about sitting quietly and breathing deeply. It can be gardening, running, painting, or any activity that can allow your mind to be still.

A simple breathing exercise you can try is called box breathing. You can try this on the go, but I find it works better when sitting comfortably.

- Inhale and count to four
- Hold your breath and count to four
- Exhale and count to four
- Count to four
- Repeat

What could you do to bring meditation into your life?

Affirmations

I have filled my Facebook and Instagram feeds with positive accounts. These accounts regularly post positive quotes or affirmations. An affirmation is an assertion that something exists or is valid and can be used to manifest your ideal life or situation. I have affirmation cards stuck on the walls of my office, on the side of my computer screen, and in my bathroom. The amount of times I have been stuck and then look up to see the correct affirmation for me at that moment is extraordinary. I have a set of affirmation cards that I use by randomly pulling one out, and when I considered starting this book, the affirmation I saw said, "Say yes to new adventures!"

You can use different affirmations for many reasons. Here are some I use:

You can totally do this

Do what makes your soul happy

You are exactly where you need to be

Your darkest day is only 24 hours long

Make it happen

I am unstoppable

Write down your favourite affirmations, or make some up:

....

....

....

....

....

....

....

Crystals

I have loved crystals since I was a teen. I think I still have a moonstone ring I bought when I was 13. Not only are they beautiful, but they have many healing properties. When I was in the midst of my grief a few years after Warren died, my friend Karen bought me a rose quartz pendant. I put it on and immediately felt a warmth cover my chest. Within an hour, the crystal shattered, and the heat went away. Rose quartz is connected to the heart chakra and helps heal the heart from emotional wounds.

There are many crystals used in healing, so I suggest you find the ones that suit your needs. For example, I currently have several selenite lamps and towers in my house to help clear negative energy and enhance the calm in my living spaces. I also have rose quartz next to my bed and have given my boys various crystals for their rooms.

Selecting your crystal is intuitive. I find that in a box of crystals, the one I need will make itself stand out.

What are your favourite crystals?

What crystals could you use to help unblock negative energy in your life?

Spiritual healing

I was recommended a spiritual healer (InsideOut Spiritual Healing) by my friend Simone in 2019. I had never seen one but was very open to the idea. I have been spiritual my whole life and believe we are all connected energetically. Additionally, I have powerful intuition and faith in myself.

Before my first meeting with Penny, I was a little nervous, only because I knew it would be a very emotional experience. However, I was immediately put at ease with Penny's warm and calming personality. We talked a lot, I cried a lot, and I released more than I could ever have hoped.

As a Shamanic Healer, Penny delves deep into your subconscious to locate and take out any blockages that no longer serve you, and raises your vibration. Through my sessions, I have physically felt the release of these blockages and felt lighter and calmer once finished. We have cut cords to people, brought in light, and released negative emotions.

I now call Penny a friend, and she is part of my retreat team.

Have you ever tried spiritual healing? How did it make you feel?

Do you have an area of your life that feels stuck?

Is there something from your past that you feel you need help letting go of?

....

....

....

....

Fiji Retreat

I now understand the saying 'retreats change lives.' I was lucky enough to go to the Ultimate Girls Week Away in February 2020, just before COVID hit. This was the first retreat I have ever been to, and I can honestly say it changed the course of my life. Along with over 200 women from around the world, I was immersed in a bubble of love at Plantation Island Resort on an island off the coast of Fiji. The location was stunning, and the people surrounding me were full of joy and love. We enjoyed many different workshops to help guide us and bring us back to our feminine self, as well as art workshops, healing hubs, massages, and fun nights, including karaoke. There were tears, and there was laughter – an incredible amount of laughter – delicious food and a sense of belonging. A highlight was meeting Elizabeth Gilbert, author of *Eat, Pray, Love*, and listening to her wisdom in her two keynote addresses. I even danced on the beach with her after an evening market. I have a photo of myself and Liz, after she did a spontaneous watercolour workshop with me, stuck up on my office wall to remind me of my time there.

On the first day of this retreat, I realised I had found my tribe. I have always had dear friends, but there was something different about this small group of women. We somehow found each other and immediately connected. We were from all walks of life but identified with each other through shared stories, wicked senses of humour, and a genuine, immediate connection. We set up a group message and still communicate through that regularly. Since then, these women have supported me in life and business, and I am incredibly grateful to have found them.

I never truly understood the power of women supporting women. Growing up, I was shown not to trust others, to be by myself, and always be wary. For me, this was so detrimental. I used to be on guard when I met people. I now open myself up and believe the right people are finding me for a reason. This could be as a learning or teaching experience.

I love my tribes, old and new, and know that they have my back.

If you don't feel like you have found your people, try joining local clubs or groups. Of course, it's far more difficult making friends as an adult, but you only need to give it a go to realise we are all looking for a connection.

Have you ever been on a retreat?

....

....

....

....

Write a list of retreats or types of retreats you would like to go on?

....

....

....

....

Emotional Detox

Sara, one of the beautiful souls I met in Fiji, has been an incredible support since returning home. Sara runs the Living Your Truth Tribe and is a fantastic healer. I participated in her Emotional Detox program, which included timeline therapy, hypnotherapy, a whole lotta tears, and just as much laughter!

The timeline therapy allowed me to go back to the first time I remember feeling different emotions such as anger, fear, and sadness. I was put into a deep and relaxed state through Sara's calming words and imagined myself floating above my life's timeline. I visualised the line on a page with different years or events marked on the bottom. When I found the right place, I would imagine myself dropping down to that time in my life and visualised the event. I was able to see in my mind's eye that most of the times I felt these emotions, I was not actually involved. It was happening around me, not to me.

These events included my father leaving, my brothers' deaths, and other issues I had growing up. I came out of this program far more in tune with my true self and found I could easily break free from those feelings and leave them in the past where they belong.

Write a list of events in your life that you may need help letting go of:

Have you ever tried hypnosis? What did you use it for? Did it help?

What might you use hypnosis for in your life?

Journaling

I have always enjoyed writing, and journaling is one part of how I have freed myself from negative thoughts and was integral to writing this book. I had haphazardly started before Fiji, but it was specifically during the first Elizabeth Gilbert keynote address that it became clear that this needed to be a consistent part of my life.

During the keynote, we started by writing letters to Love. Here is a brief example of this letter:

Me: Dear Love, I need you today.

Love: I'm right here. Tell me what you need.

Me: I am feeling stuck. I need guidance on (you can write whatever you think you need).

Love: Think about why you are feeling this way. Can you see a way to move past it?

Me: I could try (this is where the answers start falling out of you).

Love: Yes, that could work. I am here whenever you need me. Just ask.

I always found the answer within. Love merely guided me. These letters are basically a conversation with the kindness inside you. All you need is to permit yourself to find them. By writing to Love, I calmly responded to my own questions with the answers I needed.

Other things I have done in my journal include doodling, writing affirmations, business ideas, and dear diary type of writing. It's been fascinating looking back over the past year's words to see how much I have grown.

You don't need a fancy journal; you could use a notebook or anything you already have at home. I like to carry a small pencil case with various pens and highlighters to help bring some colour to my journal.

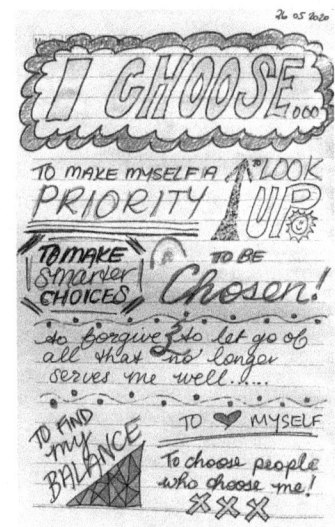

A page from my journal.

In writing this book, which has brought up so many past wounds, I gave myself permission to write openly. I have bared my soul on these pages, and it has been an incredibly cathartic experience. I don't expect everyone would enjoy writing a book but write something, anything. Getting your thoughts out of your head and onto paper is an excellent step in self-healing.

Try writing a letter to Love:

> Healing takes courage, and we all have courage,
> even if we have to dig a little to find it.
>
> **- Tori Amos**

Alternative Healthcare

Although I am not at my ideal weight and don't exercise as much as I should, I do take steps in taking care of my body. The most consistent thing I do is see an osteopath regularly. I have a sedentary job, sitting at a computer for up to 12 hours a day. It's tough on the body and mind. My osteopath has helped me understand my body and has given me the tools I need to get through my workday. I visit every four weeks, or more often as necessary. My osteo Georgia (and previously Meg) is also great to talk to, and we have lovely conversations, leaving me much happier than when I arrived. I look forward to my sessions, even though they may sometimes be physically painful. I try to use breathing techniques to get through the painful treatments.

I also regularly have a massage. Find a masseuse that suits you, whether it's one of the local venues at a shopping centre, a massage school, or remedial massage, among many others. I spend this time relaxing and clearing my thoughts. The benefits of massage, and human touch in general, can include easing tension and helping to reduce stress and anxiety. I am a big advocate of enjoying a massage and do so as often as I can afford.

List other alternative treatments that you would like to try:

What would you use them for?

Clairvoyants, mediums and tarot readers

I know some people are sceptical of these, but I have always believed in the power of intuition and energy. The various people I have seen are only ever given my first name with no other details, and I sometimes bring jewellery for them to hold. Since Dave passed away, I have seen five different people, including the world-renowned John Edward, who did a reading for me on Gold FM in Melbourne. He mentioned things about Dave that were simply impossible for him to know, like me babysitting Dave's youngest child the weekend before my reading. John also said Warren, our cousin Troy (who passed in 1988), and an old friend of Dave's (who passed around 1986) were all with Dave. I could picture all four sitting together talking about cars and motorbikes. If you are interested in listening to my reading by John, go to https://tinyurl.com/johnedwardreading (around the 3:30 mark if you want to jump straight to my reading). When you listen, he mentions the name Stephen, who I now know to be the friend of Dave's mentioned above. Also, listen out for the mention of dads! When he talks of somebody being thrown from a vehicle, it is my cousin Troy, who was thrown from his motorcycle and killed. I wish I could think fast enough at the time to realise who he was talking about but the emotion was quite intense.

Another medium told me that Warren was there, holding Dave's hand as he passed, which brought me great comfort. She mentioned nicknames, events, and many other things that showed me Dave was there with us. In addition, this lady knew I had a necklace in my handbag, a necklace Leonie gave me which contains Dave's ashes. After listening back to that reading, the list I wrote is ridiculously long as there was so much information she needed to give me.

Each has brought me peace in knowing my angel brothers are OK. They have all given me facts about my life that others would never know and have guided me in my life's path. I don't take the future visions as gospel, nor do I live my life following what they say; I simply like to hear what comes up as it helps me see I am on the right track.

If you were to see a clairvoyant, what would you want to ask about?

Career: _____

Family: _____

Loved ones who have passed: _____

Love life: _____

Health: _____

Other: _____

_____

Numbers

Again, there may be some sceptics out there, but angel numbers have been popping up for me in droves over the last 18 months. 111, 1111, 222, 333, 444, 555, and 1016 (the time of my birth) are shown to me every day. I may be working for a couple of hours and look up to check the time, and it's 2:22 pm. In Fiji, I didn't sleep very well, and every time I woke, I picked up the phone only to see an angel number. I woke multiple times each night and saw them EVERY SINGLE TIME! I believe my guides send me signs, and I love that I see these.

For details on what these numbers mean, a simple search online will show you.

Search the meanings for the following angel numbers and write them below:

111: _____

222: _____

333: _____

444: _____

555: _____

666: _____

777: _____

888: _____

999: _____

000: _____

Other: _____

_____

_____

_____

Thriving in a Pandemic

Although my healing started before the pandemic of 2020 and beyond, I evolved exponentially throughout that year. I separated from Andrew in early February, and I think we would both agree that we have a much better relationship now.

My time in Fiji, as mentioned previously, was the inspiration I needed to move forward in my life. I created a new business, Artfulness Retreats, after being so inspired by the Fiji retreat, the women there, and of course, Liz's keynotes.

In April 2020, I filmed an episode of The Chase Australia, which was aired in July. I was finally able to share that I had won with friends and family. My phone pinged at me non-stop throughout the airing and after, with good wishes and congratulations. It was an exciting experience, and I loved every minute of it. When we were chosen for the show, we had to come up with something interesting to say in our introduction. I, of course, couldn't go past telling the story of fainting while skydiving!

In August, my half-sister Cheryl found me. We now know we are not related but have formed a strong bond, and I look forward to seeing her again. Cheryl has her own story, and I hope connecting with me has helped her fill in the blanks a little. I feel like we were meant to meet now, not years ago. Had I not met Cheryl, I would not have done the DNA test and found out another truth about my life.

In September, Andrew left the family home, and I started my life as a single parent and woman. It's the first time I have lived by myself. With shared custody, I get two weeks each month to myself and am enjoying the freedom of finding myself again.

I also joined retreat school throughout the year and did a business masterclass with the local council. Monash Business Awards have since nominated me for a micro-business award for Artfulness Retreats.

I know 2020 was very difficult for many, but it was like an awakening for me. Finally, I found the time to come back to myself.

How did 2020 make you feel?

....

....

....

Can you think of any positives that came out of 2020?

....

....

....

Artfulness Retreats

The idea for this business came about in the first minutes of Elizabeth Gilbert's first keynote in Fiji. After starting Art Classes Australia and going through my healing journey, I found I wanted to help others find calm and creativity in their own life. I have recently run my first retreat, and the buzz I got out of creating a safe and calm space for my participants to immerse themselves in creativity and meditation was so rewarding. I have found a new passion, and I look forward to sharing more of my knowledge and experience as my business grows.

> You can't calm the storm, so stop trying.
> What you can do is calm yourself.
> The storm will pass.
>
> **- Timber Hawkeye**

REFLECTIONS

All of the above has helped me and may also help you. We are all unique and have different energy. I hope you have found the tips helpful and can integrate some of them into your own life. There are always pathways to choose from; it's just a matter of what path you want to go down to make changes.

It takes only one step to begin your journey, so what are you waiting for? It's time to create your own beautiful life.

> She was beautiful, but not like those girls in the magazines.
> She was beautiful, for the way she thought.
> She was beautiful, for the sparkle in her eyes when
> she talked about something she loved.
> She was beautiful, for her ability to make other
> people smile, even if she was sad.
> No, she wasn't beautiful for something as temporary as her looks.
> She was beautiful, deep down to her soul. She is beautiful.
>
> **- F. Scott Fitzgerald, The Beautiful and Damned**

FURTHER SUPPORT SERVICES

Beyond Blue – Provides information and support to help everyone in Australia achieve their best possible mental health.
www.beyondblue.org.au   1300 22 4636

Lifeline – 24/7 free telephone counselling service.
www.lifeline.org.au   131 114

Headspace – An online platform where you can access group chats, online communities and get 1:1 direct support for mental health issues.
www.headspace.org.au

MensLine Australia – 24/7 counselling and resources for men in crisis.
www.mensline.org.au   1300 789 978

SANE – Mental health information and referral service.
www.sane.org   1800 187 263

Kid's Helpline – 24/7 counselling service for kids and young people.
1800 551 800

1800 RESPECT – 24/7 national sexual assault, domestic and family violence counselling service.
1800 737 732

Child Abuse Prevention Service – 24/7 family support, abuse prevention, and community education services.
1800 688 009

The Salvation Army – 24/7 Salvos telephone counselling service.
www.salvos.org.au   1300 363 622

Parentline Australia – Support, counselling, and parent education.
www.parentline.com.au   1300 301 300

Relationships Australia – Relationship support services for individuals, families, and communities.
www.relationships.org.au   1300 364 277

Me and Leonie in 2020 at one of the two Elton John concerts we went to together.

The day I met and had a reading on Gold FM by world-renowned medium, John Edward, in 2017.

My Fiji tribe – Sara, Me, Amy, Sarah, Rachelle, Donna, and Bron (missing from this pic is the lovely Janeen), February 2020, just as COVID was starting.

Me and Sara, from Living Your Truth Tribe, in Fiji, 2020.

Pure happiness on my face during the Ultimate Girls Week Away retreat in Fiji, 2020.

I had always wanted to see dolphins in the wild, ever since I missed out on the visit to Monkey Mia in 1988. The tour guides hadn't seen any dolphins for a month, but we were lucky enough to spot them on our day out during the retreat in Fiji. So grateful.

Me on The Chase Australia, 2020.

Janeen, who I met in Fiji, sending support during the airing of my episode of The Chase Australia.

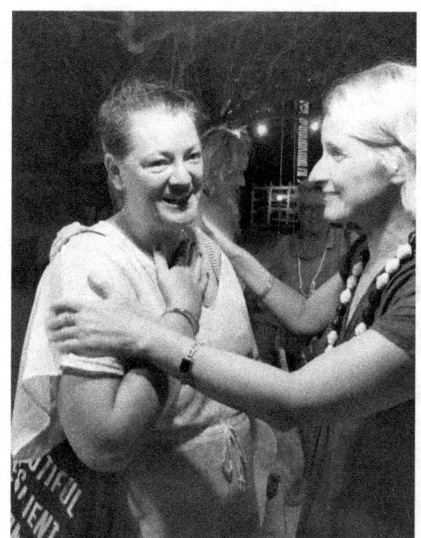

I first met Elizabeth Gilbert at the dessert bar one night at the retreat in Fiji in 2020. We then had this beautiful moment at the night market after her keynote earlier that day. Her story of losing her partner to cancer resonated so much with me and we talked briefly before dancing the evening away with a small group of women on the sand.

Elizabeth Gilbert and me after she joined my spontaneous art workshop with some of my tribe, her aunt, and her cousin.

About the Author

Sharon is a graphic designer, art teacher, retreat owner, and author of *Unmasking the Past*. She lives in Melbourne, Australia with her two teen boys and an adorable Maltese-Shih Tzu, Buddy. She is also a sister, an aunt, a friend, and a business owner – your everyday middle-aged woman.

Sharon works out of her home studio and has successfully run Sharon Westin Graphic Design since 2011, Art Classes Australia since 2019, and Artfulness Retreats since 2020. She's a life-long creative who hustles to get shit done to build the life she desires. Recently, Sharon has found a passion for helping others get back to their creative self.

Writing her first book was the next exciting stage of her life, and she already has ideas for a second. To stay up-to-date on the progress of *Unmasking the Past*, follow on Facebook, www.facebook.com/UnmaskingThePast.

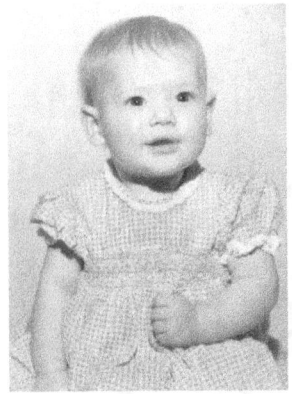
Strawberry blonde, aged around 10 months.

With a cigarette…! Aged around 18 months.

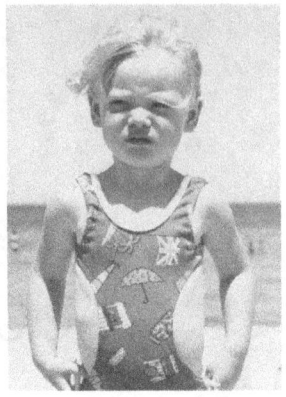
Those that know me will recognise this face! Aged two.

Me, drinking apple juice from a bottle, with my cousin Jenni, aged around two.

Sitting on our pinball machine, aged around two to three.

Apparently, I demanded my gorgeous long hair be chopped off, aged three to four.

Another cigarette!! I remember being allowed to take a drag. Aged around six.

I look at this photo and think 'there's a lot going on in that young mind.' Aged around eight.

Dressed up, aged 16.

I am so happy here, at Sue's house, aged 16.

At my boyfriend's house, after my family was evicted from our home, aged 17.

Ready for a job interview, at Mum's house in Hastings, aged 19.

Skydiving, aged 20. I passed out moments later and awoke upon landing.

On my wedding day, at Catani Gardens, St Kilda. Photo by Joe Surace.

On my honeymoon in Thailand, 2004.

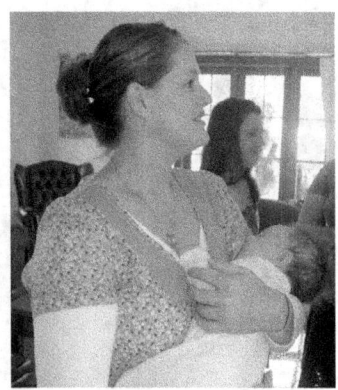

With Connor, at Baz and Emi's wedding in 2005.

Baby Mitchell in my arms, Christmas Day 2007.

With my boys at Frankston beach, 2008.

Mitch and me at his 6th birthday party, 2013.

Me, Connor, and Mitch at Lake Mountain, 2014.

I still can't believe I managed to complete Stadium Stomp at the MCG in 2015. I lost 20kgs before the event.

Left: Connor and me at his first concert, AC/DC in 2016.

Below left: Me and Connor at Castlerigg Stone Circle in Cumbria, England, 2016.

Below: A dream come true. I finally made it to the Louvre in Paris, 2016.

Above: Connor, me, and Mitch, on my 40th birthday at St Kilda beach, 2016.

Left: Mitch and me at the Elton John concert in 2020, singing in the rain.

Just another selfie in 2016. I'm usually behind the camera so I take a lot of these!

Heartfelt thanks

My boys, Connor and Mitchell, are my joy and have brought a richness to my life that I cherish. They are intelligent, loyal, funny, and empathetic, and I am so grateful to be their mum. They will never truly know how much I love them and how thankful I am for their support, always, but especially over the last 18 months.

Although our marriage has ended, Andrew has been, and continues to be, a big part of my life. He has supported me through motherhood, starting my businesses, and has always backed me. I am very grateful to have him in my life.

I briefly mentioned Leonie in the dedication of this book, but there is so much more to add. Leonie is one of the strongest people I know and one of the best mums. She continues to forge through all her hardships and has been such a strength to me. We talk regularly and help each other through every problem, big or small. She never judges me, and I can speak openly and honestly to her. Dave and Leonie's kids, Katelyn, Sarah, Brendon, and Daniel, are a credit to them both and also support me in their own ways. I am incredibly proud to be their aunty.

My in-laws have been a great support to me over the last 20 years and I am so grateful to have them in my life. My kids are also fortunate to have such wonderful grandparents, aunties and uncles.

I first met Nick in my early 20s, when we worked a few doors apart in Elsternwick. We hit it off immediately, but we went on our own paths as life went on. Reconnecting again in 2019, we realised our friendship was still solid. I am so grateful for his honesty, clarity, and level-headed responses to my many upheavals. It also doesn't hurt that he is one of the funniest and most brilliant people I know and owns two adorable Labradors!

Jodie (Gorg) and I met in 1989, in year seven. She has been a dear friend ever since and was my bridesmaid. Jodie has always been an ear for my troubles and has been a fantastic friend, giving pragmatic advice whenever needed.

Oogie Boogie! Ben and I also met in year seven. He has been a champion of my business, offering advice and also becoming a client. But, more importantly, Ben has been a great mate. He continuously checks in with me and offers support. Before my overseas trip in 2016, he gave me a copy of Dr Seuss' *Oh, The Places You'll Go* that I have in my office to remind me of our friendship and the possibility of new journeys.

Simone is a mum I met when Connor started prep. Although we have been friends all that time, she has been a great support to me these last few years. She checks in to see if I'm OK and always offers a hand, even though her own hands are full. Love ya, chick!

There are many people in my life that I am thankful for. It would take another book to thank everyone personally, but please know, I am so grateful for everyone in my life. You all hold a very special place in my heart.

> Happiness is the consequence of personal effort. You fight for it, strive for it, insist upon it, and sometimes even travel around the world looking for it. You have to participate relentlessly in the manifestations of your own blessings. And once you have achieved a state of happiness, you must never become lax about maintaining it. You must make a mighty effort to keep swimming upward into that happiness forever to stay afloat on top of it.
>
> – Elizabeth Gilbert

Helpful Chakra Guide

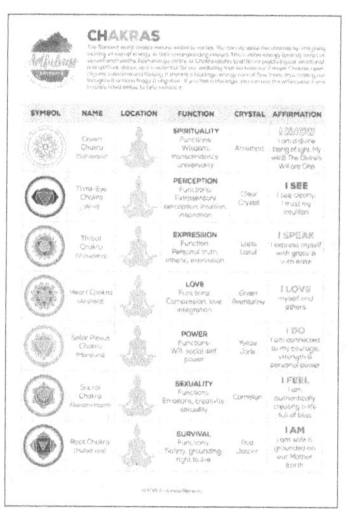

Get your printable Chakra Poster to show you the functions of each chakra, help you understand where you may have blockages, and what affirmations and crystals can help you clear those blockages.

To get your poster, email
sharon@artfulnessretreats.com.au

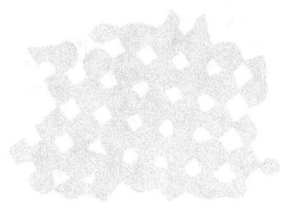

The Beginner's Guide to Creating Abstract Art

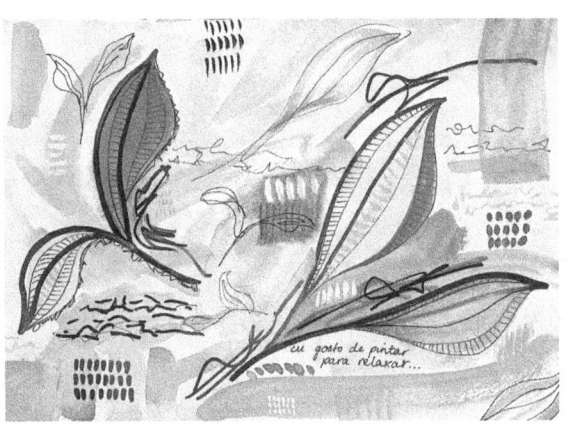

Grab your complimentary Art Tutorial that will help you bring out your inner creative with this simple to use guide. Art is a great way to bring calm into your life so don't let your fear of artistic ability hold you back.

To access your tutorial, email
sharon@artfulnessretreats.com.au

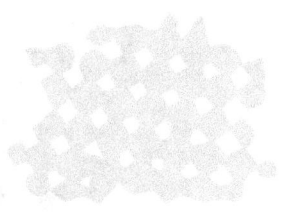

Unique Retreat Experiences

Stay up-to-date with all upcoming retreats at artfulnessretreats.com.au

Readers of this book can get on a VIP list to be the first to hear about our unique retreat experiences before the general public.

To become a VIP, email sharon@artfulnessretreats.com.au

SHARON WESTIN

An engaging and inspiring speaker, Sharon Westin is a graphic designer, art teacher, retreat facilitator and the author of *Unmasking The Past*.

As a life-long creative, Sharon has the tips and tricks to bring your creativity back, helping to block out the noise of your busy life.

Her traumatic life experiences have strengthened her resolve and taught her to maintain a solid self-belief to strive to create a life of her design.

Years of spiritual inner work have enabled Sharon to overcome anxiety, depression and a victim mindset, and rediscover what lights her fire; creativity and helping people.

BECOME THE CREATIVE YOU FORGOT YOU WERE
- Remember the creativity you had as a child
- Removing the self-doubt to see your potential
- Weekly ideas to bring creativity back into your life

FLIP THE SCRIPT TO OVERCOME THE VICTIM MINDSET
- Understanding why you feel like a victim
- Releasing your negative thoughts and fear
- Unmask your past to create the future you deserve

FROM NEGATIVE TO POSITIVE
- Discover what blocks your positivity
- Mastering the daily habits for success
- Embracing alternative ways to heal your mind

Contact Sharon at
sharon@artfulnessretreats.com.au
to enquire about her speaking at
your event, availability and rates.

Products

Cards for Creativity

52 ideas to bring creativity into your life.

These cards aim to get your right brain active, giving you inspiration to bring creativity into your life each week.

To purchase, visit https://artfulnessretreats.com.au/store

Products

Watercolour Palette

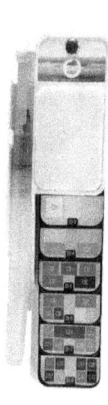 

The Artfulness Watercolour Palette is easy to use and less messy than traditional paint sets. It is designed to be portable so the artist within can create whenever, wherever. All you need is water!

The compact set comes with 33 colours and one refillable brush, a washable sponge and a palette, yet is small enough to fit in your hand. The nontoxic paints are great for adults and kids alike, and the refillable paint brush means no messy spills!

To purchase, visit https://artfulnessretreats.com.au/store

Products

6-piece Refillable Paintbrush Set

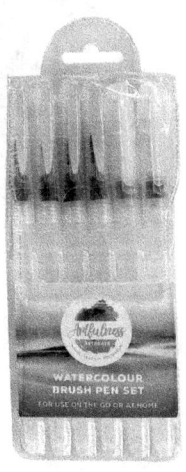

The 6-piece refillable paintbrush set includes portable water brush pens with a soft, plastic barrel to allow you to control the flow of water with a simple squeeze.

Each brush has a nylon tip, making them durable, and allowing them to keep their shape. They are also very easy to clean by running them under water. Simple!

Brushes come in sizes 01, 02, 03, 04, 07, & 10.
To purchase, visit https://artfulnessretreats.com.au/store

www.ingramcontent.com/pod-product-compliance
Lightning Source LLC
Chambersburg PA
CBHW071734080526
44588CB00013B/2021